The Mysterious and Prophetic History of Esau Considered, in Connection With the Numerous Prophecies Concerning Edom [Signed J.H.]

MYSTERIOUS AND PROPHETIC

HISTORY OF ESAU

CONSIDERED,

IN CONNECTION WITH THE

NUMEROUS PROPHECIES CONCERNING EDOM;

IN A SERIES OF

COLLECTIONS FROM THE OLD AND NEW TESTAMENT,

SHEWING THE NECESSITY OF A RETROSPECTION FROM THE

LAST TO THE FIRST, AS A

SURE KEY TO THE SCHEME OF PROPHECY.

———

Esau is Edom.—GEN. xxxvi. 8.

———

LONDON:

PRINTED FOR J. G. & F. RIVINGTON,

ST. PAUL'S CHURCH YARD,

AND WATERLOO PLACE, PALL MALL.

———

1837.

7³¹.

LONDON:
GILBERT & RIVINGTON, PRINTERS,
ST. JOHN'S SQUARE.

PREFACE.

THE Biblical student must be allowed to lament that the department of Prophecy has worn such a repulsive aspect to the world, as not only to leave it without the assistance, which literary conversation, and the statement of various opinions, usually give ; but also to produce a feeling of discouragement among those who are really friends to prophetic investigation. Nevertheless, after a research into the obscured path of Prophecy has once been cautiously ventured upon, and a view towards the opening prospect of conviction has become discernible, the solitary examiner finds that it cannot be quitted.

And what other pursuit, it may be asked, in the whole range of human intelligence, is so worthy either of the aspiring or of the self-inquiring mind, as the endeavour to clear the way towards the infolded meanings of our life-giving Scriptures, the fruits of which may then become our own? The sentiments of an able theologian upon this subject are so favourable to the pursuit, that a passage from his much valued work must here be quoted.

"A like labour of the mind, with a similar exercise of our faculties, is requisite, in order to obtain knowledge, both human and divine : this is the very purpose of that Being who confers the blessing; we must seek to find, and knock to have it opened. From discoveries hence made, we learn what a number of latent truths are to be found in the Scriptures; and when these, upon examination, are observed, they afford more inward satisfaction, and are more conducive to faith, than if they were superficial and self-evident. They likewise increase our regard for the Scriptures; for the more we discover of latent design and wisdom in an object, the greater will be our veneration, and the stronger our faith [1]."

[1] Gray's Key to the Old Testament.

What a still more modern writer has said, in respect to the conviction which must follow mathematical demonstration, may also be brought to bear upon the conviction which we ought to feel, when we see a remote Prophecy fulfilled in our own days.—"I need not add that, whenever such mathematical reasoning can be applied, it affords the only means of rendering doubt absurd, and dissent ridiculous."

J. H.

Close, L ———.
May, 1837.

CONTENTS.

CHAPTER I.

PRELIMINARY.

"In the latter days ye shall consider it perfectly."

JEREMIAH, ch. xxiii. v. 20.

The evil spirit conspicuously portrayed in the Holy Scriptures, p. 2.—Change
effected in the moral government of the world by the fall of man, p. 2.—
Increase of worldly knowledge in the present day, calling for, and encoura-
ging, a farther and deeper investigation of the Bible, p. 3.—The New
Testament throwing light upon the temporary obscurity of the Old Testament
prophecies, p. 5.—Sir Isaac Newton's opinion of prophecy, p. 5.—Instance
of this in the explanation given by subsequent revelations, of the wickedness
of the old world, and prevalent idolatry of the new, p. 7.—Opinion of St.
Chrysostom stated respecting St. Paul's especial communications to the Ephesians, p. 9.—Consideration of the predestinated children, p. 10.—The wheat
and tares, p. 11.—The multiplied conception, and the sorrow consequent upon
it, p. 12.—Cain and Abel, p. 13—The substitute, provided for murdered Abel,
requisite as a revival or perpetuation of the good seed, p. 14.—Three different
seeds in the world, p. 15.—Cain's progeny specially marked, p. 16.—The cause
why the worship of God did not preeminently succeed in the new world, traced
in the nature of the three sons of Noah, p. 17.—From their progeny arose the
predicted empires of Daniel, p. 18.—The wickedness of these nations only to be
accounted for upon the principle of Satan's ascendancy in the new world, as
well as in the old, p. 19.—Gradual but increasing spread of the good seed,
p. 20.—Their long oppression, p. 21.—Instanced in the destruction of the

B

IN the history of the beginning of this world vouchsafed to us in the Holy Scriptures, the vivifying power and word of the Deity are indeed shown to preside, but He is himself nowhere expressly portrayed. His exemplification is in his works. But the evil spirit, which disturbed the original plan of the new world, is rendered conspicuous, in the very first scene of it, by the portrait of the intellectual serpent. He is therefore meant evidently to be the great object of visual attention, and serious consideration. Moreover, in the continued chain or series of revelations in the New Testament, the same being is farther and more fully portrayed, and explained to be Satan and the Devil, in a state of rebellion against God. He is described also as having revolted angels at his command, and as having been able by their assistance to wage war in heaven. This seems at first a subject too high for us to investigate ; but the inspired volume propounds the subject : later revelations are promised, and we are told to " search the Scriptures," which will give evidence of prescience, and thereby both sanction our belief, and reward our diligence.

The manner of the fall has been clearly related to us. We find that the plan of the human world was altered by withdrawing the paradisaical state ;

and that new sentences were consequently pronounced by the Deity himself. These sentences must be supposed to affect all flesh, to have been put into immediate execution, and also to have been in operation ever since. The New Testament indeed proves that the great inimical serpent, so plainly offered to our consideration in the Holy Scriptures, will be in action to the end of the world. Our Saviour frequently adverts to his (Satan's) being temporary Prince of it, and the whole context of Scripture declares the same. He is constantly at work in the matter of his rebellion, which constitutes the warfare of the world so often spoken of in the Bible.

There is at present a new, and almost unaccountable avidity, to dispense the fruit of the tree of knowledge, among the lower orders of the people, including women and children. It is true that the dispensers of wholesome and salutary books have also been awakened, and this defensive principle proves the controversy, the decided, though almost invisible *enmity*, now existing between two different parties. Yet, as we have already seen "spiritual wickedness," and patrons of infidelity, "in high places," shall we leave the fair warnings of Scripture concerning them unexplored, or at least unattempted, amidst this great increase of *worldly* knowledge?

"The general impression which the Scriptures leave upon our minds is this: that God desires his

creatures to entertain a reverential love of his goodness, as well as a reverential awe of his justice, in
his administration of the moral government of the
world, and does not call upon us to abandon our
notions of right and wrong, or the results of that
gift of reason, which he has permitted to survive
the fall[1]."

After considering, therefore, the miraculous manner in which the Scriptures have been immutably
preserved and handed down to us by a people who
are themselves a standing miracle, the contempla-
tive and piously disposed mind may feel sanctioned
in proceeding, with sobriety of apprehension, to
examine some of those parts of Holy Writ, which
have hitherto been permitted to exercise the scep-
tic and amuse the witty; while the sacred volume,
in no way concerned for the cavilers, continues its
prophetic course with simple narratives, extraordinary portraits, and an open acknowledgement of
mystery; yet with the information that there is a
prescribed term, after which, the mystery will be
unfolded. The prophecies are given to us as a
well-fraught mine, and the Book delivered by God's
own hand, in the fifth of Revelations, is sealed with
seven seals, which can only be opened by the
slain Lamb, that is, by the elucidations of the New
Testament, published after the atoning blood had
been shed. It is evidently the intent of prophetic

---

[1] Sumner's Apostolical Preaching, p. 69.

language, not only to veil the subject which it portrays till the time of fulfilment, but often long after it, that they of an unconscious world may at a distant time look back, and by the help of history, and a common chronological table, ascertain with precision, and contemplate with awe, those fulfilments, which had for a long appointed time lain unobserved.

Proceeding, therefore, upon that presumption, the endeavour will be to shew, that the course of this world, from the time of the fall to that of the flood, and from thence to the present time, has been regularly and incontrovertibly, though abstrusely, given to us in the Bible; but that the development of those parts of the Old Testament which seem obscure, will depend upon our close inspection and right apprehension of the latter revelations of the New Testament.

According to Sir Isaac Newton, " The design of God, when he gave the prophecies, was not to gratify men's curiosities by enabling them to foreknow things, but that, after they were fulfilled, they might be interpreted by the event, and his own providence, not the interpreter's, be manifested thereby to the world."—" The event will prove the Apocalypse, and this prophecy, thus proved and understood, will open the old prophets; and all together will make known the true religion and establish it."

From the above quotations, we may conclude

that the superior mind of Sir Isaac Newton had, in the spirit of integrity, gone over the whole of the Apocalypse, and though unable to elicit any thing definite from the reserved parts, had imbibed from the matured communications as much information as secured his entire confidence in the remaining divisions of the scheme; while he at the same time foresaw, that however pregnant either the early narratives or chronological prophecies may be, no part of them will be allowed to become manifest till the exactly appointed hour. And, by the way, this restricted progress of development, may in some degree account for the partially permitted shutting up of the Scriptures[1], and the free circulation of such contumely as is usually cast upon the humble readers of Revelation, but which, under Providence, may only act, as the cold winds do, in checking a too forward vegetation.

The promising view which Sir Isaac Newton has given of the usefulness of collating retrospective prophecy, is so far justified by the great probability of its truth, and the possibility at least, if not the feasibility, of our proving it by a diligent investigation of both Testaments, that the sober mind may rationally attempt the task. It may hope, by such a comparison of the apparently recondite prophecies, and seemingly simple narratives of Scripture, to be able eventually to discern the foredoomed cause

---

[1] By the Roman Catholics.

or permission of many of those extraordinary events and fulfilments, which have silently taken place in the world, since the first ordinances issued by the Deity himself, upon the great event of the fall. For, unless we go back to that imbittered fountain-head, and take exact account of every sentence then pronounced, and every narrative then given, in order to trace the after consequences from their *beginning*, we should still be utterly at a loss to account, upon any given or definite principle, for the acknowledged corruption of the old world, and that spirit of rebellion and " evil imaginations," which survived the penal infliction of the flood, and began again in the notable first empire of the New World, Babylon. This idolatrous state having arisen among the offspring of Noah, a man approved of by God, a " preacher of righteousness," and who survived for 350 years after the descent from the ark, must of itself arrest our attention. How could such a dereliction take place under the superintendence of the Deity, and his chosen agent Noah ? The striking anomaly of the case requires investigation ; because common sense is at a stand, when, after the purgation of a wicked world, no visible amendment succeeds. But confidence in our holy Creator inclines us to *re-consider* the state of the case from the *beginning*, in order to see whether the cause of this *defection* is not enveloped in his own *communications*. Now, by the subsequent elucidations of the New Testament, we find that the serpent of

1

the third of Genesis, so strikingly, so strongly portrayed to us, was the great inimical spirit, Satan, in a state of rebellion against God.   And we find that after his ensnarement of our first parents into disobedience by his extreme subtilty and power, he gained such an advantage by their transgression of the commandment of God, and their consequent forfeiture of the paradisaical state, as brought them within the sphere of his own rebellion, and apparently entitled him to a temporary dominion' over their posterity.   It seems indeed as if this dominion would have been complete, had not the mercy of God, and the compassion of the Saviour, determined to redeem them at an appointed time, by the shedding of that blood, which should fulfil the sentence of death passed upon them if they transgressed the commandment of their Creator.   This method of salvation however was partially kept secret until the time of its fulfilment, four thousand years afterwards.

If these suppositions are borne out, first by an investigation of the sentences passed in the third of Genesis, and secondly by the corroborations of the New Testament, we shall no longer be at a loss to account for the avowed wickedness of the old world, or the long night of paganism and idolatry, which history unfolds to us in the new, down to the time when the shedding of the Saviour's blood sealed the redemption, and set up a kingdom, the vital principle of which, though obscured, had been con-

stantly kept alive in the line of Seth, all through
the long course of the predicted empires, till the
birth of Christ, under the reign of Augustus, the
first emperor of Rome.

Having presumed that there is a line of veiled
communications, which, by a collation of the two
Testaments, may be found to give regular intimations of all the great changes and ruling principles
which have been allowed to operate in the human
world ever since the fall, it may now be necessary
to bring forward, as far as ability, brevity, and other
circumstances will permit, a summary evidence in
favour of that apprehension, and turn a retrospective view upon some earthly fulfilments, which have
taken place without our having been conscious
either of the prophecy or its accomplishment.

St. Chrysostom mentions it as a received opinion
that St. Paul made especial communications to the
Ephesians: it may therefore be useful to refer to
that epistle when treating upon the beginning of
the human world.

Adam and Eve were the first people of the covenant or Church of God. They were of one substance, and God blessed them as one, and called
their name Adam. When they brake the commandment of God, therefore, they fell from their
first estate as *one*. But we must presume that,
before the fall, their descendants were intended to
be pure and exclusive seed, as seems expressed to
the Ephesians, where it appears that a community

of celestial spirits, of the family of God, were, before the foundation of the world, predestinated unto the adoption of children, meant for an earthly course, in the flesh. So in Hebrews, ch. ii. ver. 14, "Forasmuch then as the children are partakers of flesh and blood, he also himself likewise took part of the same; that through death he might destroy him that had the power of death, that is, the devil."

EPHESIANS, CHAP. I.

Ver. 3. "Blessed be the God and Father of our Lord Jesus Christ, who hath blessed us with all spiritual blessings in heavenly places in Christ;

Ver. 4. "According as he hath chosen us in him before the foundation of the world, that we should be holy and without blame before him in love;

Ver. 5. "Having predestinated us unto the adoption of children by Jesus Christ to himself, according to the good pleasure of his will,

Ver. 6. "To the praise of the glory of his grace, wherein he hath made us accepted in the beloved,

Ver. 7. "In whom we have redemption through his blood, the forgiveness of sins, according to the riches of his grace."

CHAP. III.

Ver. 9. "And to make all men see what is the fellowship of the mystery, which from the beginning of the world hath been hid in God, who created all things by Jesus Christ.

Ver. 14. "For this cause I bow my knees unto the Father of our Lord Jesus Christ,

Ver. 15. "Of whom the whole family in heaven and earth is named."

Here, then, I cannot but repeat, from the Epistle to the Hebrews, "*Forasmuch then as the children are* PARTAKERS *of* FLESH *and* BLOOD, *He also himself partook of the same ;*" and, in the Ephesians, we find that these predestinated *children* have an *inheritance.* They are therefore an exclusive community ; and this is apparently the communication made by St. Paul to the Ephesians. Mr. Greswell, an author who never could have heard of the above deduction, speaks as follows of the radical difference there must be between the wheat and the tares of the parable in St. Matthew. " The tares (or zizans) were the children of the wicked one, (*that is of the evil one,*) and the enemy who sowed them was the devil; which being the case, as the children, or plantation of the evil one, are thus personally opposed to the children of the kingdom, the plantation of the Son of Man ; and as the sower, or father of the one, is personally opposed to the sower, or spiritual father of the other, whatever may be farther denoted by these zizans, in contradistinction to the wheat, thus much will be certain—they cannot be those who are designed for an immortal inheritance, by virtue of a certain relation to Jesus Christ; they must be persons, who are destined to be excluded from such an inheritance [1]."

After the foregoing anticipation concerning different communities of people, from the New Testament, in which there are many such notices, we return to the early communications in the third of Genesis. We there find that, after the ensnarement of our first parents, the earth is cursed, and Satan, the intellective serpent who deceived them, is cursed also. But it nowhere appears that this strong and rebellious spirit is banished from the earth. On the contrary, God tells him that there shall be enmity between his seed and the woman's seed. This incidentally proclaims two different seeds as *dwellers upon the earth*, and, in corroboration of the view here taken, the very next sentence of punishment, consequent upon the fall, informs the woman that she will be subject to a *multiplied* conception. The words are, " I will greatly *multiply* thy *sorrow* and thy *conception;* in sorrow thou shalt bring forth children." Thus sorrow *precedes* the conception, and also takes place upon the birth of children. Adam is alike doomed to *sorrow* " all the days of his life," and the *same word* denotes the *sorrow* of each. But this kind of sorrow, denounced by the same word on each, cannot mean the bodily, the exclusive pains of child-birth, because in *that* the man has no part. In fact, the term

[1] Greswell on the Parables.

sorrow does not so properly belong to bodily pain as to mental suffering, and *sorrow* is the penalty inflicted alike upon both. Now, what sorrow could exceed that of Adam and Eve, if they found that, by the *multiplied conception,* other and baser seed would now be sharers in the newly organized world, which had been originally destined solely for themselves and their own exclusive posterity?

The *intimation* of good and bad seed, with *enmity* between them, is followed up in the very next chapter with the *information,* that the two first-born male children of Adam and Eve were at such *enmity,* that the wicked brother slew the righteous one. This *original* difference between them *must* be apprehended, because God, who knew the inward spirits of all flesh, while he was favourable to the offering of Abel, would not accept that of Cain, before any earthly crime was attributed to him.

The distribution of good and bad seed in the flesh is often related in the Old Testament, and incontrovertibly described and illustrated by our Saviour himself in the thirteenth chapter of St. Matthew, 25th verse. " But while men slept, his enemy came and sowed tares among the wheat, and went his way [1]." If this plain explanation is considered,

---

[1] The strength of the argument here adverted to, is contained in our Saviour's own interpretation of the parable to his disciples in which he expressly states that it is *really* himself that sows the good seed, and that it is *really* Satan that sows the bad seed.

with reference to the ordination of God concerning the multiplied conception, as set forth in the third of Genesis, we shall then see a specific and probable cause for the extreme *sorrow* of Adam and Eve, when the *multiplied conception* was denounced. And to show us that the slain brother Abel was *intended good seed from heaven,* God himself, with the knowledge of the woman, supplied another good seed to fill up his place. " For God, hath appointed me another seed instead of Abel, whom Cain slew," Genesis iv. 25. If, for a series of reasons which are yet to come, it is admitted, on the other hand, that Cain was of *bad seed,* the ascendency of his progeny in the world after the fall appears to be foreshown by the Deity himself, when he says to Cain, in mitigation of his avowed favour to Abel. Genesis iv. 7. " And *unto thee shall be his desire, and thou shalt* RULE *over him.*" Still, this did not assuage Cain's *enmity,* and, for more reasons than are explained to us, he effected the murder of his brother. And our Saviour corroboratively says, in speaking of Satan, " *he was a murderer from the*

V. 36. "And his disciples came unto him saying, Declare unto us the parable of the tares of the field.

V. 37. " He answered and said unto them, *He that soweth the good seed is the Son of Man ;*

V. 38. " The field is the world; the good seed are the children of the kingdom; but the tares are the children of the wicked one ;

V. 39. " *The enemy that sowed them is the* DEVIL *;* the harvest is the end of the world ; and the reapers are the angels."

BEGINNING." If God, moreover, had not supplied
another seed of the *divine nature*, Cain, (being the
first born,) would, after the death of Abel, have become chief inheritor of this world, according to
the signification of his name " ACQUISITION." But
Adam and Eve, having acknowledged their beguile-
ment by the serpent, brought up their children to
sacrifice unto the Lord; and never manifesting any
disposition to proceed in their disobedience, evidently became objects of divine mercy; and, in
proof of this, God appointed, exclusive of Adam's
common descendants, that *other good seed*, Seth,
in whose line their redeeming Saviour was eventually to be born. This lineage, pure and especially appointed, must be considered as abhorrent
of Cain's descendants, and there must be a spiritual *enmity* between them; while Adam's seed forms
apparently a third description of the human race.
And it is far from a strained inference to suppose,
that, when God supplied a substitute for murdered
Abel, he saw that it was requisite to be done, as a
revival or perpetuation of that good seed, which
Satan's device had sought to destroy, and put out of
the world, as an obstacle to his own pre-eminence.

Cain was " *wroth*" with God, and " went from
his presence" into another land, where he built a
city. Can we suppose that, under such a state of
guilt, wrath, and banishment from the presence of
the Lord, Cain would bring up his children to " *call
upon his name ?*" When we read, therefore, Genesis,

vi. 26. " *Then began men to call upon the name of the Lord*," or to " *call themselves* by the name of the Lord," or, as others translate the passage, " then *men profaned* in calling themselves by the name of the Lord," do we not at once see that the last translation is the true one, and that Cain's seed here receive *specifically* the term of *men*, which when emphatically applied in Scripture, distinguishes them from those who are termed the *sons of God?* Thus there may have been three different and distinct seeds in the world, the children of Adam, the children of Cain, and the children of Seth. There are, however, in the sacred books only two genealogies. That of Adam includes Seth, and the sons and daughters which were born to him after Seth. No mention is made in it of Cain, and the New Testament concurs in the exclusion. His genealogy stands alone in another chapter. Cain is therefore negatively ejected, and it is naturally to be expected that his much marked, and distinctly separated progeny, will receive some specific term by which they may be described in Scripture. Accordingly, in the next chapter but one, the sixth, we come upon such complete evidence concerning two different sorts of people dwelling upon the earth, that it cannot be called presumptive, but *positive* and *incontrovertible*. One community is denominated, the children of *God;* and the other, the children of *men*. The spiritual difference also between them was so great, that God forbade intermarriages between them; and the disobedience of that command introduced so much evil, *enmity* and violence, that *" God said, My Spirit shall not always strive with man for that* HE ALSO *is flesh* [1]."

Genesis, ch. vi. ver. 13. " And God said unto Noah, The end of all flesh is come before me; for the earth is filled with violence through *them :* and behold I will destroy them with the earth." This was effected by means of the deluge, in which eight persons only were permitted to survive. Among these, Noah, a preacher of righteousness, was, while in the ark, the patriarchal conductor. The Sacred Records, however, allow us to perceive that, after the descent from the ark, the worship of God did not pre-eminently succeed in the New World. This remains to be accounted for. Shem, indeed, is first named of Noah's sons, because in his line it was obscurely intimated that the darkly-promised bruiser of the serpent's head should be born. But Ham, the irreverent Ham, is also named before his elder brother Japhet. This, with some other circumstances, indicates that Ham has a certain mysterious pre-eminence. It is not, however, a holy pre-eminence, because he is twice announced as the father of Canaan, one who is cursed without any alleged cause, and his whole race shown to be diabolical, and objects of Divine vengeance. In Ham's line also began Babylon, the

---

[1] The *multiplied conception* could introduce Satan's seed into the flesh.

fountain head of all the idolatry and heathenism
which deluged the following empires. We cannot
therefore suppose that Ham was *good seed*. He
had, nevertheless, been allowed precedence over
his elder brother Japhet, and from thence might
be prognosticated, what the ruler of the New
world would be. We may perhaps also recognize,
in the three sons of Noah, a perpetuation of the
three supposed stems which peopled the Old World,
the children of Seth, the children of Cain, and the
children of Adam. In this case, the elder would
again stand last in point of precedency, but if
such be the intended arrangement of Scripture, we
must conjecture that there are reasons for it with
which we are not yet openly made acquainted. Of
these three seeds however was the New World re-
plenished, according to God's permission ; and from
their progeny arose *the predicted empires* of the
prophet Daniel, the ferocious emblems, and con-
demnatory descriptions of which fully show, by the
hand of the inspired penman, that they *were not
with God*, but were, as Cain had previously expressed it, *hidden from his face*.

The earth had been cursed ; Satan also had been
cursed, when, by means of the transgression, he had
induced Adam to forfeit his first estate, and fall
from being sole possessor of the world. Who then
was so likely to prefer a claim, or seize on the
vacated dominion, as the tempter, a dominion too,
which he had himself achieved ? We may consider

him to have received God's permission or acquiescence, when, in the ninth chapter of Genesis, after
blessing Noah and his sons, God addressed, it may
be, an unknown party, at the 7th verse, saying,
"*And* YOU, *be ye fruitful, and multiply; bring forth
abundantly in the earth, and multiply therein.*"
Likewise, in making a covenant with Noah and
his sons, not to destroy the earth again by a flood,
God seems covertly to make the same promise to
another party that is with them.

Ver. 9. "And I, behold, I establish my covenant
with you, and with your seed after you.

Ver. 10. "And with every living creature that is
with you, of the fowl, of the cattle, and of every
beast of the earth with you ; from all that go out of
the ark, to every beast of the earth.

Ver. 11. "And I will establish my covenant with
you; neither shall all flesh be cut off any more by
the waters of a flood ; neither shall there any more
be a flood to destroy the earth.

Ver. 12. "And God said, This is the token of the
covenant which I make between me and you, and
every living creature that is with you, for perpetual
generations."

Unless, indeed, we acknowledge the ascendency
of Satan in the New World, how can we account
for the idolatry of Babylon, the cruelty of the Persians, the tyranny of the Romans, and the specified
rebellion and blasphemy of the Saracenic dominion?
To which must be added the corruption of the Jews

by the seduction of their intermarriages with the *forbidden nations.* This transgression of the divine command introduced the Satanic seed among themselves, so that the priests of Baal were at times very numerous even in Jerusalem. But redemption had been ordained, and, although the time appointed was long and secret, the vital course of the *good seed* never ceased, till at length, after the crucifixion had completed the atonement, the kingdom of Christ, though small in its beginning, and opposed by Jews, Romans, and afterwards Saracens, began to be in its operation like the leaven which a woman hid in three measures of meal till the whole was leavened. And, notwithstanding all the open and all the disguised opposition, which that kingdom meets with, it is still on the increase, with every prospect of final victory over the strong adversary[1], though not till after a long pilgrimage, and severe conflict towards the end. The prospect of this happy consummation seems even now opening upon us in the wide and general dispersion of the Holy Scriptures.

[1] " But the multiplying brood of the ungodly shall not thrive, nor take deep rooting from bastard slips, nor lay any fast foundation. For though they flourish in branches for a time: yet, standing not fast, they shall be shaken with the wind, and through the force of the winds they shall be rooted out. The imperfect branches shall be broken off, their fruit unprofitable, not ripe to eat, yea, meet for nothing."—*Wisdom of Solomon,* ch. iv. 3, 4, 5.

" For horrible is the end of the unrighteous *generation.*"—*Ibid.* ch. iii. 19.

Some account of the long continued oppression of Adam's fallen children, fallen under the dominion of Satan, may be traced throughout the Psalms, where they supplicate for divine assistance, which is promised, if they continue their course with patience to the end.   Profane history also may show the common reader, that the four greater empires of Daniel were for ages devoid of any knowledge of the revealed God.   This they could not have been, had not the first empire, Babylon, rebelliously departed from the righteous preaching of their patriarch Noah.   Idolatry and the worship of Satan were *again*, by the *striving* of *men against God*, introduced into Babylon, and circulated throughout all the other empires, but not without the knowledge and notice of Scripture, which after the fall of Babylon thus warns the Jews of their approaching fate by the hands of the Romans.   Isaiah, ch. xiv. v. 29.   *" Rejoice not thou, whole Palestina, because the rod of him that smote thee is broken:* for out of the serpent's root shall come forth a cockatrice, and his fruit shall be a *fiery flying serpent."*

Ver. 31.   " Howl, O gate ; cry, O city ; thou, whole Palestina, art dissolved : for there shall come *from the north* a smoke, and none shall be alone in his *appointed times."*

The Romans, *coming from the north,* utterly destroyed Jerusalem in the year 70 of the Christian æra, and, according to the generality of commentators, the pagan Roman empire is prefigured in the Revelations by a *red dragon* or *serpent*. Red or scarlet is in Scripture the beacon colour, or type, by which people are warned of sin in an object so characterized, and Rome has always officially adopted this colour. In the above quotation from the Old Testament, it appears that a *red* or *fiery flying serpent* would, after the fall of the city of Babylon, *come from the north*, and destroy the polity of Palestine. History, by a common chronological table, will show the fulfilment of this prophecy, proved by a collation of the Old and New Testaments. It will also demonstrate, according to the corroborations which will be brought forward, the certain prevalence, and widely extended circulation, of the Satanic spirit, all through the predicted and pagan empires of Daniel, till the great encounter with Christianity, after our Lord's atoning death, and the promulgation of the Gospel, which lowered Paganism from the seven hills of Rome.

REVELATIONS, CHAP. xii.

Ver. 7. " And there was war in heaven : Michael and his angels fought against the dragon ; and the dragon fought and his angels,

Ver. 8. " And prevailed not ; neither was their place found any more in heaven.

Ver. 9. " And the great dragon was cast out, that old serpent, called the Devil, and Satan, which deceiveth the whole world : he was cast out into the earth, and his angels were cast out with him."

1

" Upon what rational and philosophical grounds the possible existence of created beings superior to man can be disputed, it is not easy to imagine. To allege their invisibility as an argument against it, would be to deny the being of a God. Is the impossibility of conceiving how immaterial spirits can receive or impart ideas, pleaded in bar of their existence? It does not follow from our ignorance of the mode that there is no mode. . . . . With regard to the Scriptures, every one must own, that in numerous passages, both sentimental and historical, the literal sense, at least, manifestly implies that there are angels of different orders. . . . . He who admits that the first human pair fell from their original state of righteousness and felicity, cannot rationally doubt the possibility of so mournful a change taking place respecting beings of a higher description in the creation, or of its seeming right in the sight of the Divine Being to permit such a change. . . . . It ought not then to appear strange that the apostle Jude, notwithstanding he does not state the nature of the temptation, should describe some of the angels as not ' keeping their first estate,' and as being ' reserved in chains under darkness to the judgment of the great day ;' nor ought there to seem any improbability in the declaration, as it strikes the reader at first view, that requires a departure from the natural sense of the statement, in order to avoid an absurdity.

" Assuming, then, that there are apostate spirits who have rendered themselves thus depraved and mi-

serable, it certainly will not be thought incredible that
they should be as much inclined, as the wicked of an
inferior order among men, to plunge others into similar guilt and wretchedness, or to obstruct their emer-
ging from that horrible situation. . . . . Nothing, it is
probable, would prevent their endeavouring to rea-
lize these fell desires, except the want of power;
and whether the existence of this power be not
possible in its own nature, or the exercise of it to
a certain extent be not permitted by the Almighty,
for his own glory and the good of his creatures in
general, (and their expediency to these ends cannot
be disproved, or even disputed, without controver-
ting the propriety of suffering moral evil to exist,)
are the points that come next to be examined.

"Impossible as it seems for us to attempt to influence beings of a higher order with any rational
hope of success, the reverse does not seem in itself
equally impossible. Our ingenuity and labour are
not unfrequently employed with effect, in aiming
to render the inanimate creation, the animal world,
and even our fellow-creatures, subservient to our
views. Is it incredible, then, that created beings
who excel us in nature, should possess means, if
allowed to use them, of practising at least, whether
successfully or otherwise, upon the same subjects
as ourselves, and upon us likewise? . . . . . .

"There are some particulars recorded concerning the heathen oracles of old, which, if true, can
scarcely be accounted for without admitting the in-

tervention of superior spirits; and these must have been *evil*, considering the character of the persons assisted, and the objects of that assistance. The occasional interposition of good and friendly angels in the affairs of men, and the fact of their some-times exciting ideas in the human mind, are gladly acknowledged, though the mode in this case is not more conceivable than in the case which concerns the agency of the apostate angels.

"The probability, then, as well as the possibility, of temptations arising from evil spirits being in-controvertible, there seems no reason why the statements in Scripture on the subject should not be understood literally, and considered both as proofs and as illustrations of the point in question, particularly when their number, variety, and cir-cumstantial minuteness, are taken into view. Alle-gory, however proper for poetry, and the senti-mental parts of a work, seems utterly incompatible with the nature, simplicity, and use of history, ex-cept in the reflections which occasionally accom-pany the narrative.....

"We may easily conceive, if the different kinds of darkness were under the control and direction of evil spirits who acted in concert, (as the scrip-tural expression 'rulers of the darkness of this world,' seems to intimate,) what powerful engines they might become of doing mischief. Nor is it impossible, or even improbable, that they should possess this power in some cases, and to a certain extent. It is not indeed credible that such a dominion either has been, or could be, committed to men. . . . . . . He that perplexed and deceived the human mind at first, ' that caused sin to enter into the world,' and thus ensured the existence of natural evil in all its forms, may reasonably be viewed as a principal, in the local and temporary prevalence of ignorance and delusion, of wickedness and misery. Though it be not easy to imagine that bad men, (who chiefly propose to themselves personal gratification and advantage, whose acquaintance with each other, and common interest, depend upon contingencies, whose connexion must be exceedingly limited, being liable to prevention, interruption, or termination, by means of a thousand circumstances,) should at any time every where unite against the cause of holiness and felicity, much less continue that union through successive generations ; yet the same difficulties do not occur in supposing a confederacy thus universal and durable among the powers of darkness, *they having always, since their exclusion from heaven, formed one vast society, with the same views and interests,* having a regular established government among them, together with easy means of communication, and never being subject to death. At the same time, though human beings that are wicked cannot be supposed to have formed, or to be executing a plan of general co-operation throughout the world, for the vile purpose of introducing, continuing, or promoting mental darkness, in a moral or religious sense,—though they cannot any of them be thought capable of acting as rulers or even as prime agents in this detestable undertaking,—yet they may act under the leaders above mentioned, incautiously or willingly lending themselves as subordinate instruments, to ' blind first their own minds and hearts,' and afterwards those of others. *It is certain that the ostensible authors, abettors, and defenders of intellectual and moral darkness, whether acting upon a small or upon a large scale, whether for a few years, or for ages, are in many instances known to have been men. Still it is utterly improbable either that they would have thought of it, or propagated it with so much zeal and success, had they not been secretly taught, excited, or assisted by invisible principals.*"

[1] Burnside on the Temptations of Evil Spirits.

CHAPTER II.

THE METALLIC IMAGE.

" There is a God in heaven that revealeth secrets, and maketh
known to the king Nebuchadnezzar what shall be in the LAT-
TER DAYS."

DANIEL, ch. ii. v. 28.

Probability that some particular prophecies may for a season have been mistaken, and applied to objects which they only partially resembled, p. 30.—
The clearer subsequent development of such prophecies of great use in giving
interest to the Scriptures, p. 31.—The Metallic Image of the book of Daniel
generally considered to be a compendium of the four empires of Babylon,
Persia, Greece and Rome, p. 31.—Strange omission of the *Saracenic* in this
system, p. 32.—Spirit of idolatry in ancient Babylon, p. 33.—Satanic influence
circulating in all the four great empires, p. 34.—Nebuchadnezzar's dream,
in Daniel's fourth chapter, containing an infolded prediction of the approaching fall of the empire, p. 34.—Improbability that Daniel should portray
a *falling* dynasty under the symbol of a *rising* beast, p. 35.—Though the *last*
beast of the series must synchronize with the *last* empire of the Metallic
Image, it does not follow that the *first* empires should have commenced at the
same time, or been duplicates of each other, p. 35.—Probable reason why the
lion should be suffered for a season to be identified with the golden head,
p. 36.—Different scales laid down for the compendiums, p. 37.—The æra of
the conquest of Babylon by Cyrus, the basis of Pagan chronology, p. 38.—
Seventh chapter of Daniel, p. 38.—The lion shown to tally best with the
silver emblem of the Metallic Image of the twofold state of the Medes and

---

IT may, before examination, be thought improbable that any of the prophecies of Daniel, which have passed through so many ages, and so many able hands, without being perfectly construed, should meet with a better fate in modern times; but a *temporarily closed* book seems to have been intimated to the world in the 4th verse of his last chapter ; *" But thou, O Daniel, shut up the words, and seal the book, even to the time of the end: many shall run to and fro, and knowledge shall be increased*[1].

[1] To signify the Christian period, (apprehended to be two thousand years,) there seem to be several terms and phrases used in the Old Testament, such as " the latter days," " the last days," " the time of the end," and " the last time of the end."

Daniel wrote five hundred years before the birth of Christ, and above two thousand before the present time. In respect to him, therefore, the Christian period may very appropriately be called *" the time of the end."* When Daniel had concluded his prophecy

We are now greatly in advance towards *the time of the end,* when the *shutting up of the words,* may cease, and divine *knowledge* be thereby *increased.* And if, in our present research, an eminent portrait in prophecy can be found, that was, by almost general consent, attributed to a certain object, which indeed in several features it seemed to resemble, but that, four hundred years after the existence of that mistaken object, another equal in importance and magnitude arose, which much more completely corresponded with the portrait, shall we not become aware of the pregnant state of early prophecies, and the great use that may be derived from

and desired to know the meaning thereof, he received the following answer, "*Go thy way, Daniel, for the words are closed up and sealed till the time of the end.*" After the subsequent course of five centuries, we of the Christian period received, at the beginning of that period, a Revelation from the hands of St. John, whose fifth chapter relates that a momentous book, sealed with seven seals, was delivered from the throne in heaven, and that it could only be opened by the *slain Lamb.* This being then accomplished by the slain Lamb, proves the period of the opening to be the Christian æra. We are now far advanced in this period; the seven seals therefore of that book having been opened, the shutting up of the words may cease, and Divine "knowledge be increased" in this "*last time of the end.*"

To a search after this Divine knowledge we are certainly encouraged by the first verse of St. John's preface, as well as by the 10th verse of his last chapter, where it is said, "*Seal* NOT *the sayings of the prophecy of this book,* for the time is at hand." The Revelations are therefore evidently thrown open to the humble investigator.

a studious retrospect of them from the first book of Scripture to the last? It is, in fact, evident, from what has been already promulgated, that we have much yet to learn concerning the course of this world. Allusion is often made to the dark nations of the globe, but they still remain a mystery to us. The docile mind and pious heart may indeed be satisfied of the divinity of the Scriptures by those internal results of content and happiness, which always attend upon such as are guided by their precepts. But what is to be the help of those who, having received what is called a liberal education, (without religion,) have no taste for the Bible? Ought they not to be warned that " it is not want of proof, but want of investigation, that makes the infidel?" If therefore a fair fulfilment of an eminent prophecy, but a fulfilment which has never been observed by the world, can be brought forward to their view, will it not at once relieve them from the erroneous idea that the Scriptures are void of interest, and at the same time prove how redundant in prescience the ancient prophecies may be found?

The Metallic Image of the book of Daniel is generally looked upon as a compendium of the four empires of Babylon, Persia, Greece and Rome, which rose in succession upon that part of the earth which is evidently marked out as the site of prophetic representations from the given station, Ancient Babylon. And, in point of time, the scheme reaches to the end of the world, when the God of heaven will set up a kingdom which shall never be destroyed. Now, this looks like consummation; but in this system, the Roman empire is considered to be the last, and this conclusion was very natural to those commentators who did not live to see the fall of the Roman empire, and the rise of another upon the same predicted space; which, from its duration, extent, strength, and universality, appears to have greater claims to the title of empire than some of those to which it has been awarded. Alexander the Great reigned but ten or twelve years, and his swift career of conquest, over nations which he did not live to cement together, is so accurately described in a subsequent vision in the eighth chapter, that his identity *there* cannot be doubted. Moreover it is added that, when he became strong, his great horn was broken. Now, is it probable that one short reign, transient conquests, and an immediately broken horn, would be symbolized as one of the fundamental empires of the Metallic Image, to the exclusion of the Saracenic dominion, which, including the caliphates, was of the continuance of eight hundred years?

In addition to this improbability, if Alexander's brief conquests were symbolized as one of the great empires of the Image, there would be three distinct and distinguished portraits of his *one* broken horn, the first in the second chapter of Daniel, the second in his seventh chapter, and the third in his eighth chapter. This is certainly not probable, because it involves the supposition, that this comprehensive prophet leaves at the same time the great Saracenic empire without *one,* in his compendiums. In his eighth chapter, the "*king of Grecia*" is accurately and individually described, both as to his beginning and ending. Can the great Antichrist Mahomet then be left without notice ? The compendiums given, and the events related, in the book of Daniel, show that his chapters, and the visions contained in them, are in general chronologically placed ; and a well-known land mark, ancient Babylon, is given as the station from which the prophetic scheme *at first* sets out.

Nebuchadnezzar's dream of the Metallic Image is the first instance given, and although, by means of Daniel's interpretation, it made the king of Babylon sensible of the almighty power of the God of Israel, it appears in the third chapter that he soon after set up a golden image, which, by proclamation, was to be worshipped by all the public functionaries, as well as by all the indiscriminate multitude, of his dominions. This elaborate record exhibits the unconquerable spirit of idolatry which ever reigned at Babylon, the first named city of the New World after the flood. And the first distinguished monarch of that city was Nimrod, whose name signified REBELLION. We find also in the fifth of Zechariah, which appears to be a prototype chapter, that wickedness was trans-

D

ported to, and settled in, the land of *Shinar*. This chain of hints in the Old Testament appears to be afforded for latter observations, when, by retrospect, we may be enabled to take up a clew from the beginning, which, if well followed through the purposely obscured paths of prophecy, and compared with history, may lead us to the knowledge of that Satanic influence, which circulated in all the four great empires of the predicted part of the earth, and was destined to encounter Christianity towards the end.

In less than a century after Nebuchadnezzar's dream, the Babylonian empire fell before the Persians, and of that fall Nebuchadnezzar himself seems to have seen a type in his second dream in the fourth chapter, where the great tree was to be hewn down by command of the *Holy Ones*. From the solemnity with which that second dream is ushered into the world, addressed to all people, nations, and languages, that dwell in all the earth, it is but reasonable to infer that it contained the *infolded* prediction of the approaching fall of the empire, which took place in the reign of Belshazzar his son, and while Daniel was yet alive. Let it be remembered, however, that, even after the Persian empire had risen to eminence, Babylon was still the capital city, the original point from which the prophetic scheme was marked to take its course. The system of the Metallic Image, therefore, suffers no interruption or deprivation by taking the lion, the

first of Daniel's four beasts, for the *Persian* empire.
The handwriting which came forth, and warned
Belshazzar that God had numbered his kingdom
and brought it to an end, was in the last year of
his reign. Was it then probable that Daniel, who
lived to witness the fulfilment, would, in a dynasty,
which was so very near its close, portray the *sinking*
empire as a *rising* beast? Besides which, the 17th
verse expressly declares all the four beasts to be
future. " *These great beasts which are four, are
four kings which* SHALL *arise out of the earth."* After
the above verse, will it not be more consistent with
the intent of prophecy, and more according to the
order of succession, to apprehend that Daniel would
rather give the first beast of the series as an emblem
of the *coming* conqueror, than mean it to be a
retrograde duplicate of the *old* and *falling* golden
head?

There is besides no necessity that, because the
last beast of the series *must* synchronise with the
last empire of the Metallic Image, they must therefore all have commenced at the same time; or the
first empires have been duplicates of each other.
The golden head had served to show the station
from which the prophetic scheme set out, but that
plain and necessary information having been afforded, prophecy, according to its known and acknowledged nature, becomes devious, being con-
structed only for future developments. And perhaps it was requisite in the court of Babylon to

guard against any perception of a *conqueror* in the lion, by allowing that beast to be construed as synonymous with the golden head. This was an error which nothing but prescience could at that time detect; and thus might the Babylonians remain unconscious that Daniel had in the lion prefigured their approaching conquest by the Persians, for Daniel *told the vision and published the matter*.

Cyrus, having by marriage united the two kingdoms of the Medes and Persians, then subdued Babylon, and formed that empire, which the modern historian would naturally suppose to be represented by the *first* of Daniel's four beasts, because he has lived to see that there *did* arise, *future* to Daniel's prophecy of four great empires, the Persian, the Grecian, the Roman, and the SARACENIC, which last momentous empire, if not reckoned in the scale, to which by succession it so evidently belongs, will remain without a portrait as a beast; for although the ninth chapter of the Revelations is looked upon as prefiguring the irruption of the Saracens, it by no means gives them the adequate portrait of an empire. Thus it will plainly appear that if the Babylonian empire, notwithstanding its fall, is still to be brought forward as the first of Daniel's series of four beasts, they will stand as follows, to the exclusion of the Saracenic empire from the evident compendiums.

1. Babylonian Empire.	1. Lion.
2. Persian.	2. Bear.
3. Grecian.	3. Leopard.
4. Roman.	4. Fourth Beast.
5. Saracenic.	

But if the Babylonian empire is considered as *falling*, and thus *not* taken as the first of the *rising* empires, the scale will run as follows —

Babylonian Empire falling.

1. Persian.	1. Lion, including the city of Babylon.
2. Grecian.	2. Bear.
3. Roman.	3. Leopard.
4. Saracenic.	4. Fourth Beast.

According to the first scale, the Saracenic is an unaccountable fifth empire, and in contradiction to the expounding angel at the 17th and 23rd verses of the seventh chapter, which, after these premises, will come fairly under consideration. It will then be seen that, from the striving of the winds upon the great sea, Daniel saw four great beasts or empires arise. This statement of itself indicated that it was a prophecy of that *which was yet to come* when Daniel beheld the vision; and in corroboration of this view of the subject, we may take into the account that, in Mr. Davison's lecture, founded by Bishop Warburton, it is shown that, *from the beginning of the Persian empire by the conquest of Cyrus*, a new epoch of chronology was begun.

" And this I may remark, that, as the æra of the conquest of Babylon by Cyrus is the basis of Pagan chronology[1], the point from which it begins to be clear and consistent; so the extraneous proof of the truth and prescience of prophecy takes its proportionate force and clearness from the same æra. The greater regularity and completeness of the Pagan narrative supplies a fuller comment upon the scheme of things delineated in the Scripture oracles."

It now seems proper to take a more minute survey of the seventh chapter of Daniel, in which the vision of the Metallic Image is contained; and in order that the subject may be placed more clearly before the reader's eyes, the whole of the chapter will be previously transcribed.

DANIEL, CHAP. vii.

Ver. 1. "In the first year of Belshazzar king of Babylon Daniel had a dream and visions of his head upon his bed: then he wrote the dream, and told the sum of the matters.

Ver. 2. "Daniel spake and said, I saw in my vision by night, and, behold, the four winds of the heaven strove upon the great sea.

---

[1] " Primus hic Cyri annus non solum solutæ captivitatis sed etiam totius vetustioris *Chronologiæ* basis est; et res Ebraicas cum extraneis connectit."—Marsham, Canon. Chron. Sæc. 18. p. 630. Ed. Francq.

·Ver. 3. "And four great beasts came up from the sea, diverse from one another.

·Ver. 4. "The first was like a lion, and had. eagle's wings : I beheld till the wings thereof were plucked, and it was lifted up from the earth, and made stand upon the feet as a man, and a man's heart was given to it.

·Ver. 5. "And behold another beast, a second, like to a bear, and it raised up itself on one side, and it had three ribs in the mouth of it between the teeth of it : and they said thus unto it, Arise, devour much flesh.

Ver. 6. "After this, I beheld, and lo another, like a leopard, which had upon the back of it four wings of a fowl; the beast had also four heads; and dominion was given to it.

Ver. 7. "After this I saw in the night visions, and behold a fourth beast, dreadful and terrible, and strong exceedingly ; and it had great iron teeth : it devoured and brake in pieces, and stamped the residue with the feet of it : and it was diverse from all the beasts that were before it ; and it had ten horns.

Ver. 8. "I considered the horns, and, behold, there came up among them another little horn, before whom there were three of the first horns plucked up by the roots : and, behold, in this horn were eyes like the eyes of man, and a mouth speaking great things.

Ver. 9. "I beheld till the thrones were cast

down, and the Ancient of days did sit, whose garment was white as snow, and the hair of his head like the pure wool: his throne was like the fiery flame, and his wheels as burning fire.

Ver. 10. "A fiery stream issued and came forth from before him: thousand thousands ministered unto him, and ten thousand times ten thousand stood before him: the judgment was set, and the books were opened.

Ver. 11. "I beheld then because of the voice of the great words which the horn spake: I beheld even till the beast was slain, and his body destroyed, and given to the burning flame.

Ver. 12. "As concerning the rest of the beasts, they had their dominion taken away: yet their lives were prolonged for a season and time.

Ver. 13. "I saw in the night visions, and, behold, one like the Son of man came with the clouds of heaven, and came to the Ancient of days, and they brought him near before him.

Ver. 14. "And there was given him dominion, and glory, and a kingdom, that all people, nations, and languages, should serve him: his dominion is an everlasting dominion, which shall not pass away, and his kingdom that which shall not be destroyed.

Ver. 15. "I Daniel was grieved in my spirit in the midst of my body, and the visions of my head troubled me.

Ver. 16. "I came near unto one of them that

stood by, and asked him the truth of all this. So he told me, and made me know the interpretation of the things.

Ver. 17. " These great beasts, which are four, are four kings, which shall arise out of the earth.

Ver. 18. " But the saints of the Most High shall take the kingdom, and possess the kingdom for ever, even for ever and ever.

Ver. 19. " Then I would know the truth of the fourth beast, which was diverse from all the others, exceeding dreadful, whose teeth were of iron, and his nails of brass ; which devoured, brake in pieces, and stamped the residue with his feet ;

Ver. 20. " And of the ten horns that were in his head, and of the other which came up, and before whom three fell ; even of that horn that had eyes, and a mouth that spake very great things, whose look was more stout than his fellows.

Ver. 21. " I beheld, and the same horn made war with the saints, and prevailed against them ;

Ver. 22. " Until the Ancient of days came, and judgment was given to the saints of the Most High ; and the time came that the saints possessed the kingdom.

Ver. 23. " Thus he said, The fourth beast shall be the fourth kingdom upon earth, which shall be diverse from all kingdoms, and shall devour the whole earth, and shall tread it down, and break it in pieces.

Ver. 24. " And the ten horns out of this kingdom

are ten kings that shall arise : and another shall rise after them ; and he shall be diverse from the first, and he shall subdue three kings.

Ver. 25. " And he shall speak great words against the Most High, and shall wear out the saints of the Most High, and think to change times and laws : and they shall be given into his hand until a time and times and the dividing of time.

Ver. 26. " But the judgment shall sit, and they shall take away his dominion, to consume and to destroy it unto the end.

Ver. 27. " And the kingdom and dominion, and the greatness of the kingdom under the whole heaven, shall be given to the people of the saints of the Most High, whose kingdom is an everlasting kingdom, and all dominions shall serve and obey him.

Ver. 28. "Hitherto is the end of the matter. As for me Daniel, my cogitations much troubled me, and my countenance changed in me : but I kept the matter in my heart."

Recollecting how little we know of the remote annals of the Assyrian and Babylonish empires, and bearing in mind that the æra of the conquest of Babylon by Cyrus is considered by historians as " the basis of Pagan chronology," which from his time " begins to be clear and consistent," we may surely venture to proceed so far upon that conclusion, as to compare, in search of agreement, the four beasts of Daniel, with the four empires, which *did* arise in succession *from that time*, and upon the predicted part of the earth. We may also compare the last of each of those two series with the last emblem of the Metallic Image, the iron mixed with clay, because the *last* beast, the *last* empire, and the *last* metal must be found to be contemporaneous, and to tally in their signification, if the compendiums are to be satisfactorily fulfilled. But how can the fulfilment be admitted as satisfactory if a great and celebrated empire which is known to have exceeded the other empires in point of time, is looked upon as without the pale of the compendiums, although on the same predicted ground, and although the compendiums are marked to include the last scenes of this world.

A lion couchant is at present the arms or ensign armorial of the Persian kingdom, but the lion of this series of beasts, in order to prove its title to represent the Persian state, must be found to tally better both with the silver emblem of the Metallic Image, and with the two-fold state of the united Persians and Medes, than it ever did with the golden head or empire of Babylon. Now this lion has upon his back two wings, which Daniel beheld till they were plucked. Nothing has ever been alleged as a fulfilment of this in the Babylonian empire, but, by the union of the Medes and Persians, their two separate governments or wings were, after being united, plucked, or dispossessed of their separate official functions, by the absorption of the one supreme head. The two wings, never-

theless, answer to the two arms of the collateral
silver emblem. The junction of the Medes and
Persians together with the conquest of the Babylonian empire raised the Persians to a height which
they had never attained before. Thus of the lion
it is said, "*It was lifted up from the earth, and
made stand upon the feet as a man, and a man's
heart was given to it.*" We must here recollect
that, in the apparent type of the fall of Nebuchadnezzar (or the Babylonian empire), a *beast's*
heart was given to him during his term of degradation, and the root of his fallen tree was also
bound down for a season in the earth by a band of
iron and brass; but the lion is *lifted up*, and a *man's*
heart is given to him. The breast (the *silver*
breast), is the region of the heart, and the heart is
the source of life and action to the frame. Now
the Persian kingdom appears to have enjoyed the
vital state of dominion to this day, but not one of
these attributes seems applicable to the golden
head, which is still bound down in the grass of the
earth, though apparently promised to revive again
hereafter.

The next beast, before which the Persian empire
suddenly fell, is called a bear, and characterised
chiefly as a devourer of much flesh. This intimation of great carnage seems to have been fulfilled
more evidently by Alexander the Great, than by
any other conqueror in the same space of time.
With thirty thousand men he destroyed the

army of Darius amounting to three hundred thousand. Some authors even compute that he destroyed six hundred thousand. This, together with the brief intervention of his other conquests, from the great consumption of human life with which they were accompanied, may seem worthy of record among the *warlike beasts,* although, from the short space of their duration, and from their uncertain limits, they are not admitted to a *fundamental station* in the *Metallic Image.* And this absence may perhaps be accounted for, when in the eighth chapter we read, that the individual king of Grecia *touched not the ground,* but, having a notable horn between his eyes, waxed very great, and that, as soon as he was *strong,* the great horn was broken. All this appears to be fulfilled by Alexander the Great. Nevertheless, the eighth chapter apparently refers also to events which are still future, but our present venturous research must be confined to the seventh chapter. Alexander's early and sudden death left his kingdom broken, subject to division, and eventually exposed to the approaching power of the more permanent Romans, after whose long dominion over it, the Grecian empire may be said to have raised itself up on one side, when upon the rising of the Greeks in 1261, the last Roman emperor, Baldwin the second, and all his adherents, fled, and never returned. The voice of history repeats that the Greeks then recovered their kingdom, but it was only on one side of Alexander's extensive conquests. Mr. Gibbon, among other historians, says, "The recovery of Constantinople was celebrated as the æra of a new empire. The conqueror, Palæologus, alone, and by the right of the sword, renewed his coronation in the Church of St. Sophia."—Gibbon, vol. ii. p. 325.

Even at this present time, the Greeks, although again subjected to a foreign conqueror, the Ottoman, are still acknowledged as a people, and may again be said to be raised up on one side. But no *dominion* is ascribed to the *bear* by Daniel, the great horn of Grecia having been *broken* as soon as the individual king became strong, and his kingdom being divided into four parts, as is described in the following chapter, the eighth.

But the next beast, the leopard, has *dominion* given to it, and *therefore tallies with the brass empire,* which *bare rule over all the earth.* And, in fact, the Romans did for centuries bear pre-eminent rule over all the predicted part of the earth, within the outline of the Metallic Image. The Roman empire also, like the Leopard, had four eminent heads, the two imperial heads of Rome, and Constantinople, and the two episcopal thrones of the Pope and the Patriarch of the eastern department of the empire. The above seeming to be as fair an adaptation of the leopard to the description of the brass empire and to the corresponding characteristics of the Roman empire, as can be expected from such concise emblems, I will for the present imagine the likeness to be admitted, because in the Metallic Image no correspondence is found with the bear.

The fourth beast without a name will *then* be contemporaneous with the iron and clay kingdom. And let us mark their peculiar attribute. They are both *strong exceedingly*. Now *strength* is one of the constant characteristic marks of the Antichristian party, from the predictions in Genesis concerning *Esau*, who is Edom, down to the time when all the greater prophets show that *Edom* comes into action in the last days. The Metallic Image and the four beasts are considered as compendiums, but a compendium will not allow us to exclude, from a station so clearly indicated by prophecy as the site of the Metallic Image, an extensive and perfectly Antichristian empire, which arose within its precincts, and succeeded the Roman but far exceeded that empire in enmity towards the religion, and the people, of the revealed God. It was much more inimical to the Christian church, and therefore peculiarly an object for prophetic notice, but most especially for the Christian prophet St. John, whose long neglected illustrations may possibly at last be discovered in the Apocalypse. In corroboration of this idea, we know from history that the latter course of human affairs has been quite as much subject to changes and great events, since the fall of the Roman empire, as before. The people of Christendom, therefore, are not likely to be abandoned from that time, and thenceforth remain shorn of all prophetic representations.

The feet and toes of the Metallic Image are composed of two substances so dissimilar, that, although proximate, they cannot cleave the one to the other. The iron substance is *strong*, one of the Antichristian attributes, but the other being of potter's clay, which is of a superior kind, is *brittle.* These different substances, which mingle together but are not *allowed* to cleave one to another, apparently represent two manner of people latterly forming the population of the iron empire, one of them being shown to be of that division, which in other parts of Scripture is emphatically termed *men.* Daniel ii. 43. " *And whereas thou sawest iron mixed with miry clay, they shall mingle themselves with the seed of* MEN : *but they* SHALL *not cleave one to another even as iron is not mixed with clay.* In the same manner, a Christian and a Mahometan cannot accord; and in the irreconcileable state of enmity, which ever has existed, and ever must exist between them, have we not a clear fulfilment of the above statement of Daniel, corroborated also by our own knowledge of the general and calamitous mingling of Mahometans with the conquered Christians, during the prevalence of the *last great empire, the Saracenic.* For we must remember that this empire continues, in the Ottoman dominion, up to this day, confirming the idea that, in the system of the fourth beast, there is still an Antichristian horn acting against a people distinguished by the name of saints. Now it is certain that the entrance of the Saviour into the world, and the propagation of the Gospel, called forth into notice a new manner of people, not *strong* indeed; for that quality belonged to their oppressors, nor were the Jews or the Christians in general able to stand against the military strength either of the Romans or the Saracens, but they were God's people, and therefore deserving of prophetic distinction in the compendiums.

The fourth beast and his horns appear to proceed on to the day of Judgment, but how can the Roman empire, the long vanished Roman empire, be portrayed as proceeding on to that day, when we know that the Saracenic empire, or beast, *terrible and strong*, overran, *brake in pieces*, and *stamped upon*, not only that empire, but the *residue* of the others which it contained ? And as chronology carries on the great Saracenic empire centuries beyond the existence of the Roman empire, and upon the same part of the earth, how can we consistently refuse to allow it a station in Daniel's compendiums which *reach to the end of the world ?* It came fairly in *succession* to the Roman empire, and was the most important and decided enemy that Christianity ever encountered, and, exactly as is described both in the Old and New Testaments, *made war upon the people of God.* The

E

remains also, the image of it, still survive in the
Mahometan horns of Turkey, Persia, India, and
parts of Africa. These continuing professors of
Mahometanism, these living remains of the Saracenic empire, may reach on to the day of Judgment, in the sight of the world.

Having therefore sought in vain for any reason
which can make it necessary to place the lion as
in point of time collateral with the golden head of
Nebuchadnezzar, I shall venture to change that
juxtaposition, and arrange the scale as follows, because the remains, the Image, or the horns, of the
Moslem Empire, being still in existence, may proceed on to the day of Judgment, and fulfil the
compendiums so as to evidence the truth of prophecy, while the other, the Roman Empire, having
long vanished, can be of no service in this respect.

Metallic Image. *Golden Head falling.*	*Seventh chapter, describing* *Daniel's four beasts which* WERE *to arise.*
Silver arms, Persia.	Lion with two wings, Persia. Bear, ten year's duration, no dominion.
Brass, Roman with dominion.	Leopard, Roman with domi- nion.
Iron and clay, Saracen, with ten toes. Of this kingdom it is said at the 41st verse of the second chapter, that it shall be *divided*.	Fourth beast, Saracen with ten horns, and a little horn so often described that *two* may be included.

It does not seem out of place to hint here, by

way of anticipation, that the universal empire, mentioned in the thirteenth chapter of the Revelations, is succeeded by a beast with *two* horns. Now as the Apocalypse is generally looked upon as an elucidation of preceding prophecies, we are warranted in evpecting to find in the Old Testament some prototype of St. John's two horned beast. Indeed without such a prototype we have no sanction whatever for the two horned beast, which nevertheless exercises all the power of the former beast, and on that account cannot be given up as irrelative in the system. We must therefore seek in the seventh chapter of Daniel for some intimation concerning him, when we reach the thirteenth chapter of St. John, in the Apocalypse.

CHAPTER III.

CONCERNING ESAU.

BEFORE we proceed to the consideration of such
portions of the Apocalypse, as appear to sanction
the system of prophetic interpretation adopted in
these pages, we shall dwell a little upon the character and circumstances of Esau and his descendants,
with a view to the same system. It is certain that
commentators have hitherto sought in vain for the
fulfilment of Esau's blessing, in the events which
originated in Arabia, inasmuch as it has never been
considered that he was virtually in that country;
while, on the other hand, they have not been able
to find, in the blessing pronounced upon Ishmael,
any thing that could portend the *great dominion*
which manifestly spread from Arabia. Now if it
can be shown, that, by his connection with Ishmael's
daughter, Esau was a dweller in Arabia, through

the medium of his descendants, the blessing attached
to him may thus appear to have been undeniably
realized, and the dominion promised to him fulfilled.
In order to show this, it will be necessary to examine
some transactions connected with Abraham, Isaac,
Ishmael, Esau, and Jacob, whose characters and
circumstances are more particularly dwelt upon,
than we can suppose the concise method of Scripture narration would authorise, unless they were
each the fountain head of an important lineage, the
progressive state of which was meant to be kept in
view, till time, and the explanations of the New
Testament, should prove how fraught they originally were with intimations of some of the great
events which have since happened in the world.

The descendants of the three Patriarchs of
Arabia, appear in Scripture to have been situated
as follows:—The sons of Joctan in Arabia Felix,
the sons of Ishmael in Arabia Deserta, and the sons
of Esau in Arabia Petræa. In this latter country
the ancient capital of Esau has lately been brought
to light, and this resurrection from oblivion is an
encouragement to make further researches into
his mysterious, and therefore long neglected, history.

The nation of Jacob has been the chief subject
of prophecy, and has been placed under the observation of all civilized people for some thousand
years; but to show that Esau and his nation are
also of importance, and to be held in especial

remembrance, we are warned, no less than five times in one chapter, that *Esau is Edom*, and the father of the *Edomites*.

GENESIS, CHAP. XXXVI.

Ver. 1. " Now these are all the generations of Esau, who is Edom."

Ver. 8. " Thus dwelt Esau in mount Seir. Esau is Edom.

Ver. 9. " And these are the generations of Esau, the father of the Edomites, in Mount Seir."

Ver. 19. " These are the sons of Esau, who is Edom, and these are the dukes."

Ver. 43. " Duke Magdiel, duke Iram: these be the dukes of Edom according to their habitations in the land of their possessions: he is Esau, the father of the Edomites.".

This reduplication was necessary, as several of the prophets did not begin to prophesy concerning Esau's posterity, till above a thousand years after his personal appearance upon earth; so that, without this remarkable repetition and strict evidence, the identity of Esau's descendants might have been disputed in the prototypes of the prophecies relating to the latter times; and the more especially as it will appear that his posterity, power, or nation, will at times be obscured from the observation of the world.

MALACHI, CHAP. i.

Ver. 2. " Was not Esau Jacob's brother? saith the Lord: yet I loved Jacob,

Ver. 3. " And I hated Esau, and laid his mountains and his heritage waste for the dragons of the wilderness.

Ver. 4. " Whereas Edom saith, We are impoverished, but we will return and build the desolate places; thus saith the Lord of hosts, They shall build, but I will throw down; and they shall call them, The border of wickedness, and, The people against whom the Lord hath indignation for ever.

Ver. 5. " And *your eyes shall see*, and ye shall say, The Lord will be magnified from the border of Israel."

The *eyes* of all may now *see* the ancient dwelling of Esau in Arabia Petræa, where the nature of the climate has preserved some of the sculpture of the long uninhabited city in perfection.

But Ishmael preceded Esau; he therefore must be first considered.

GENESIS, CHAP. xxi.

Ver. 9. " And Sarah saw the son of Agar the Egyptian, which she had borne unto Abraham, mocking.

Ver. 10. " Wherefore she said unto Abraham, Cast out this bond-woman and her son: for the son of this bond-woman shall not be heir with my son, even with Isaac.

Ver. 11. "And the thing was very grievous in Abraham's sight, because of his son.

Ver. 12. "And God said unto Abraham, Let it not be grievous in thy sight, because of the lad, and because of thy bond-woman; in all that Sarah hath said unto thee, hearken unto her voice: for in Isaac shall thy seed be called.

Ver. 13. "And also of the son of the bond-woman will I make a nation, because he is thy seed."

Moses has shown that Noah was perfect in his generations, and from Noah's approved son, Shem, Abraham's descent is carefully given; his promised son, Isaac, therefore, by a free woman, must be considered as one of the sons of God: but Ishmael his brother, although he received a blessing from God, is clearly marked as of an inferior nature to Isaac, even in the Old Testament.—First, by his descent on his mother's side; secondly, by his own marriage with an Egyptian, which still keeps his posterity in the line of Ham; and thirdly, by the declaration of Sarah, that he should not inherit with her son; which declaration must be looked upon as prophetical in respect to his posterity, because it is immediately approved of by the Lord, and the subject resumed with confirmation in the New Testament more than a thousand years afterwards.

GALATIANS, CHAP. iv.

Ver. 22. "For it is written, that Abraham had two sons; the one by a bond-maid, the other by a free woman.

Ver. 23. "But he who was of the bond-woman, was born after the flesh : but he of the free woman was by promise. That is, he was *promised* seed."

Ver. 28. "Now we, brethren, as Isaac was, are the children of promise.

Ver. 29. "But as then he that was born after the flesh persecuted him that was born after the spirit, even so it is now."

This appears to be positive information concerning enmity; and, at the 23rd verse, all that has been conjectured concerning a radical difference of origin seems confirmed; Ishmael is declared to be born after the flesh, while the Jews, the sons of God, are recognized as the children of the promise.

Ver. 30. "Nevertheless, what saith the Scripture? Cast out the bond-woman and her son : for the son of the bond-woman shall not be heir with the son of the freewoman.

If Sarah's declaration that Ishmael should not inherit with Isaac had only appeared in the Old Testament, it might have passed as an instance of the selfishness of a mother; but when it is thus resumed in the New Testament, it assumes a more serious aspect, and demands our attention ; for

what was in the Old Testament called the word of
Sarah, is here stated to be the word of Scripture.
Moreover, the posterity of the two brothers being
distinct in the world at this day, the fulfilment of
Sarah's prophetic declaration concerning them may
be distinctly judged of. The Jews, we see, are
still, notwithstanding their degradation, in full possession of the covenant of their forefathers, while
Ishmael's posterity, the Arabians, are more devoid
of the power to inherit with them than ever, by
their assumption of the Mahometan religion. And
thus are Sarah's prophetic words completed, and
the son of the bond-woman is *not heir* with the son
of the free woman.

And that these two predicted nations should
have been so long kept distinct from other nations,
the one under dispersion, and the other nearly continuing in its primordial station, must have been
for the purpose of finally manifesting the foreknow-
ledge of Scripture by the fulfilment of the prophecies concerning them in the latter days.

All travellers, both ancient and modern, attest
that the characteristic of the Arab is his propensity
to robbery. The characteristic of Esau remains to
be developed by the spirit of his blessing. Quit-
ting, therefore, for the present, the predatory course
of Ishmael's posterity seated in Arabia *Deserta,*
we must follow that of Isaac in the two *separated*
branches of Esau and Jacob.

Ver. 19. "And these are the generations of Isaac, Abraham's son : Abraham begat Isaac.

Ver. 20. "And Isaac was forty years old when he took Rebekah to wife, the daughter of Bethuel the Syrian of Padan-aram, the sister to Laban the Syrian.

Ver. 21. "And Isaac intreated the Lord for his wife because she was barren: and the Lord was intreated of him, and Rebekah his wife conceived.

Ver. 22. "And the children struggled together within her ; and she said, If it be so, why am I thus ? and she went to inquire of the Lord.

Ver. 23. "And the Lord said unto her, Two nations are in thy womb, and two manner of people shall be separated from thy bowels ; and the one people shall be stronger than the other people ; and the elder shall serve the younger."

It must be kept in mind that this answer from the Lord himself was given *after* the struggle, the extraordinary struggle, had taken place.

Two nations and two manner of people, that is, two nations totally distinct, and, as we shall find, totally separated for ever.

Ver. 24. "And when her days to be delivered were fulfilled, behold, there were twins in her womb.

Ver. 25. "And the first came out red, all over like an hairy garment ; and they called his name Esau.

Ver. 26. "And after that came his brother out, and his hand took hold on Esau's heel : and his name was called Jacob : and Isaac was threescore years old when she bare him.".

The posterity of Jacob and Esau became, according to prophecy, distinct from the first. After an absence of four hundred years, the nation of Jacob returned into Arabia, but found no brothers in the Edomites, the sons of Esau, who kept themselves so distinct from the Israelites, that they refused to let them even pass through their highways, and they wandered forty years in the wilderness of Arabia, without any reciprocity which could be an infringement of the prophetic declaration, that they would be *two nations* and *two manner of people.*

"*And the elder shall serve the younger.*" This is a very remarkable prophecy, because the birth-right would then be in the hands of the one that was to *serve.* As yet it is inexplicable, because in those days the birth-right was considered " as an holy thing, not only because the priesthood was annexed to it, but also because it was a privilege leading to Christ, and a type of his title to the heavenly inheritance." It was therefore an object of great consequence ; and from the *recorded struggle* in the womb, and the subsequent circumstance of Jacob's laying hold of Esau's heel in the birth, we may conceive that Jacob then laid claim to the primogenial state from which the predicted STRENGTH of Esau had, in the struggle in the womb, displaced him. Esau was born *red*, a colour never characteristic of innocence in the Scriptures, but, on the contrary, emblematic of the deepest sin ; and this colour is farther attached to him by different means, as will appear.

In Isaac the *promised* seed was to be called; and it surely has appeared, that both *bad* and *good* seed are in the world; discrimination is therefore necessary upon this important occasion. The circumstances, also, which preceded the birth of Esau and Jacob, are of so extraordinary a nature, and so laid out for observation, that our attention is immediately awakened. We certainly cannot suppose that the current of Scripture information would be arrested in its course to notice the movements of these children in the womb, unless from the movement (or *displacing*) some alteration in the primogenitureship would ensue, an alteration of vital importance, inasmuch as, in those days, the eldership and birthright conferred some mystic or spiritual benefits. We may therefore rest assured, that God would eventually bestow them where they were originally meant to be given, notwithstanding the most cunning devices of Satan, in the struggle to displace the promised seed.

Ver. 27. " And the boys grew : and Esau was a cunning hunter, a man of the field; and Jacob was a plain man, dwelling in tents.

Ver. 28. " And Isaac loved Esau, because he did eat of his venison; but Rebekah loved Jacob.

Ver. 29. " And Jacob sod pottage: and Esau came from the field, and he was faint.

Ver. 30. "And Esau said to Jacob, Feed me, I pray thee, with that same red pottage; for I am faint: therefore was his name called Edom (that is, *red*).

Ver. 31. "And Jacob said, Sell me this day thy birth-right."

There is great probability that Rebekah (who had received an answer from the Lord concerning the struggle in her womb,) would inform Jacob that he had been dispossessed of his birth-right by that struggle; and thus will all the unexplained methods of Providence be gradually revealed to man.

Ver. 32. "And Esau said, Behold, I am at the point to die; and what profit shall this birth-right do to me?

Ver. 33. "And Jacob said, Swear to me this day; and he sware unto him: and he sold his birth-right unto Jacob.

Ver. 34. "Then Jacob gave Esau bread and pottage of lentiles; and he did eat and drink, and rose up, and went his way. Thus Esau despised his birth-right."

In this manner did Esau acquire the branding name of *Edom* or *red*, by eating that same red pottage for which he sold his birth-right, confirming it with an oath; and thus Jacob either gained, or regained, the birth-right. But, independently of all inference, Jacob evidently prized the birth-right, and Esau, according to Scripture mention,

despised it; that which led to Christ was *despised*
by him; and the New Testament corroborates this
by calling him the *profane* Esau. Nor do we hear
of any instance of his piety : on the contrary,
when he sold his birth-right, we are told that he
did eat, and drink, and got up, and went his way,
without expressing any regret at having parted
with it; and, at the thirty-fourth verse of the
twenty-sixth chapter, it will be found that he took
two wives from the forbidden race, " which were a
grief of mind unto Isaac, and to Rebekah," ver. 35.

We know not the extent of Rebekah's information when she went to inquire of the Lord, nor the
result of her own reflections upon the extraordinary
struggle in the womb, and the peculiar circumstances attending the birth of these children ; but
by her subsequent conduct in resolutely excluding
Esau from his father's prime blessing, and saying
fearlessly to Jacob, when he remonstrated, " Upon
me be the curse (which you apprehend) my son,
only obey my voice," did she not prove that she
knew Esau was not eligible to receive that blessing?
For we cannot suppose that a woman of an approved race, and so far pointed out as the destined
wife of Isaac, by Divine interference, that the
sworn servant of Abraham, when he saw it, bowed
his head and worshipped the Lord—we cannot
surely suppose that such a woman, and one also
who had received an answer from the Lord concerning these children, would practise duplicity in

order to divert the prime blessing from the person, to whom, in the usual course of things, it would have belonged.

With respect to Isaac's dereliction, it must be recollected that he was old and could not see ; he therefore from the infirmities of age, forgetfulness, or undue partiality, or even from ignorance of the existing circumstances, might err in his choice of the person on whom to bestow the blessing ; but, in the fortieth verse, it is shown that upon *consideration,* he chose to confirm what he had done.

GENESIS, CHAP. XXVII.

Ver. 14. "And he went, and fetched, and brought them to his mother : and his mother made savoury meat such as his father loved."

Ver. 25. "And he said, Bring it near to me, and I will eat of my son's venison, that my soul may bless thee. And he brought it near to him, and he did eat : and he brought him wine, and he drank.

Ver. 26. "And his father Isaac said unto him, Come near now, and kiss me, my son.

Ver. 27. "And he came near, and kissed him : and he smelled the smell of his raiment, and blessed him, and said, See, the smell of my son is as the smell of a field which the Lord hath blessed.

Ver. 28. " Therefore God give thee of the dew of heaven, and the fatness of the earth, and plenty of corn and wine :

Ver. 29. " Let people serve thee, and nations bow down to thee : be lord over thy brethren, and let thy mother's sons bow down to thee : cursed be every one that curseth thee, and blessed be he that blesseth thee.

Ver. 30. " And it came to pass, as soon as Isaac had made an end of blessing Jacob, and Jacob was yet scarce gone out from the presence of Isaac his father, that Esau his brother came in from his hunting.

Ver. 31. " And he also had made savoury meat, and brought it unto his father, and said unto his father, Let my father arise, and eat of his son's venison, that thy soul may bless me.

Ver. 32. " And Isaac his father said unto him, Who art thou ? And he said, I am thy son, thy first-born, Esau.

Ver. 33. " And Isaac trembled very exceedingly, and said, Who ? where is he that hath taken venison, and brought it me, and I have eaten of all before thou camest, and have blessed him ? yea, and he shall be blessed.

Ver. 34. " And when Esau heard the words of his father, he cried with a great and exceeding bitter cry, and said unto his father, Bless me, even me also, O my father."

We are at first inclined to pity Esau, when we

read of his exceeding bitter cry; but, when we consider the context, we perceive that it could only have been excited by sorrow for the loss of pre-eminence which the blessing might have given him.

Ver. 37. "And Isaac answered and said unto Esau, Behold, I have made him thy lord, and all his brethren have I given to him for servants; and with corn and wine have I sustained him: and what shall I do now unto thee, my son?

Ver. 38. "And Esau said unto his father, Hast thou but one blessing, my father? bless me, even me also, O my father. And Esau lifted up his voice, and wept.

Ver. 39. "And Isaac his father answered, and said unto him, Behold, thy dwelling shall be the fatness of the earth, and of the dew of heaven from above;

Ver. 40. "And by thy sword shalt thou live, and shalt serve thy brother; and it shall come to pass when thou shalt have the dominion, that thou shalt break his yoke from off thy neck.

Ver. 41. "And Esau hated Jacob because of the blessing wherewith his father blessed him: and Esau said in his heart, The days of mourning for my father are at hand; then will I slay my brother Jacob [1].

Ver. 42. "And these words of Esau her elder

---

[1] Cain, the *bad* seed, slew Abel the *good* seed.

son were told to Rebekah : and she sent and called
Jacob her younger son, and said unto him, Behold,
thy brother Esau, as touching thee, doth comfort
himself, purposing to kill thee.

Ver. 43. " Now therefore, my son, obey my
voice ; and arise, flee thou to Laban my brother
to Haran;

Ver. 44. " And tarry with him a few days, until
thy brother's fury turn away;

Ver. 45. " Until thy brother's anger turn away
from thee, and he forget that which thou hast done
to him : then I will send and fetch thee from
thence. Why should I be deprived also of you
both in one day ?

Ver. 46. " And Rebekah said to Isaac, I am
weary of my life because of the daughters of Heth :
if Jacob take a wife of the daughters of Heth,
such as these which are of the daughters of the
land, what good shall my life do me ?"————These
daughters of the land, it must be remembered,
were descended from Canaan, who lay under the
curse, and into whose line Esau had disobediently
married to the grief of his father and mother.

In some respects, the separate blessings bestowed
upon the two brothers resemble each other. The
fatness of the earth, and the dew of heaven, are
alike afforded to each ; but the exceeding trembling
of Isaac, when he knew not to whom he might
have given the first blessing, proved that he considered it as of great importance. *Corn* and *wine* do

not seem things of any particular consequence in Jacob's blessing. Yet when Isaac recapitulates the blessing to Esau, he does not omit them, as if they were of minor consideration, but says, " With corn and wine have I sustained him, and what shall I do now unto thee, my son ?" The corn and wine, therefore, must be held in remembrance; and the more especially as Jacob, in the future blessing which he gives to his son Judah, adverts to wine as a part of his portion ; and our Saviour and the Jewish nation are in several parts of Scripture prefigured by the vine. We must observe also, that, when the harvest of the earth is reaped, in the fourteenth chapter of Revelations, the reaping of the earth, and gathering of the vine of the earth, are each performed by a different angel : and as these two in-gatherings are distinct, so, we must infer, are the people to whom they relate.

GENESIS, CHAP. XXVIII.

Ver. 1. " And Isaac called Jacob, and blessed him, and charged him, and said unto him, Thou shalt not take a wife of the daughters of Canaan.

Ver. 2. " Arise, go to Padan-aram, to the house of Bethuel thy mother's father; and take thee a a wife from thence of the daughters of Laban, thy mother's brother.

Ver. 3. " And God Almighty bless thee, and

make thee fruitful, and multiply thee, that thou mayest be a multitude of people;

Ver. 4. "And give thee the blessing of Abraham, to thee, and to thy seed with thee; that thou mayest inherit the land wherein thou art a stranger, which God gave unto Abraham.

Ver. 5. "And Isaac sent away Jacob: and he went to Padan-aram, unto Laban, son of Bethuel the Syrian, the brother of Rebekah, Jacob's and Esau's mother.

Ver. 6. "When Esau saw that Isaac had blessed Jacob, and sent him away to Padan-aram, to take him a wife from thence; and that, as he blessed him, he gave him a charge, saying, Thou shalt not take a wife of the daughters of Canaan;

Ver. 7. "And that Jacob obeyed his father and his mother, and was gone to Padan-aram;

Ver. 8. "And Esau seeing that the daughters of Canaan pleased not Isaac his father;

Ver. 9. "Then went Esau unto Ishmael, and took unto the wives which he had, Mahalath *the daughter of* Ishmael, Abraham's son, *the sister of Nebajoth*, to be his wife."

Thus Esau is shown to be incorporated with Ishmael, who, though blessed of God as a great nation, has been carefully noted as born after the flesh, and who married in the line of Ham. Ishmael's country also is much marked, both in Scripture and in profane history : while the mountains of Seir, bordering upon his territories, remain such immoveable monuments of Esau's early station, and one of his last appellations *Edom*, that no difficulty can arise upon that subject. Great care also is taken to mark to us the different principles upon which the two brothers contracted their very different alliances. Jacob acted from pure obedience, and Esau, in the two first instances, from grievous disobedience. Afterwards, indeed, when he saw that Jacob was approved of by his parents, because he took not of the Canaanitish women, he also, in order to obtain some share of approbation, took another wife, but even she was not within the line of the heavenly inheritance; from which we may infer that there was a *positive bar against the connection*.

This third wife was Mahalath the daughter of Ishmael, of whom Sarah had declared that he should not inherit with Isaac. All Esau's wives are thus shown to be without the pale of the heavenly inheritance; and upon what account can we suppose that Scripture would be so particular in mentioning who Esau's three wives were, unless it was at the same time to denote in what line his posterity was to be considered?

This daughter of Ishmael is also twice mentioned as *the sister of Nebaioth*, Ishmael's eldest son; which peculiarity of twice adverting to her brother's name, may be a leading intimation of what is most

7

probable, that Esau's descendants by her might, by way of distinguishing them from his descendants by his other wives, be termed *Nabatheans*, or Arabians. The mountains of Seir traversed a part of Arabia, and from thence might Esau's descendants by Nebaioth's sister have spread into the interior of that country, under the name of Nabatheans. These were a distinguished people in Arabia, of whom the Universal History gives the following account :—"Among the ancient Greeks and Romans, the inhabitants of Arabia Petræa and Arabia Deserta, at least the bulk of them, for many ages went by the names of Arabes and Nabatai. They extended themselves, according to St. Jerome, from the Red Sea to the Euphrates, and all the tract they inhabited was from them denominated Nabatana.—In after ages, the names of all the nations here touched upon, were absorbed in that of Saracens, which continued famous for several centuries over the eastern and western parts of the world[1]."

As far back as profane history reaches, the Arabians, that is the Edomites and the Ishmaelites, have been known as Pagans and idolaters. In the New Testament, Ishmael is strongly marked as *born after the flesh*, and a persecutor ; and Esau is described as the *profane* Esau, and *Edom*, against whom the Lord hath indignation *for ever*. On

[1] History of the Arabs, p. 248.

what account then can we conceive that the junction of two such families as those of Ishmael and Esau, should be so minutely *recorded* in the early prophecies of Scripture, unless it was for the especial purpose of exciting our attention, and warning us that the coalescence was of a portentous nature, and virtually pregnant with future consequences to the world? And as the New Testament resumes the subject with elucidations, it is natural to conclude that their descendants are actors in the predicted warfare of the Christian period. Ishmael's descendants have been obvious in Arabia to this day; and the chief[1] of the prophets show, that Esau or Edom will reach down to, and be in action during, the last times.

But, in taking up the course of Esau from the beginning, it will be necessary to examine his blessing, to see whether, from the intimations given there, we cannot find some corresponding traces of him in the world, both before and after he became obscured under that veil, which is acknowledged to exist when it is said, "How are the things of Esau searched out; how are his hidden things sought up." And in Jeremiah xlix. 10. "But I have made Esau bare. I have uncovered his secret places, and he shall not be able to hide himself."

Before the second century Esau's name was forgotten in Mount Seir and Idumæa, and in the

---

[1] Isaiah, Jeremiah, Ezekiel, Joel, Amos, Obadiah, and Malachi.

thirty-eighth Psalm he is classed with the Ishmaelites, with whom he had intermarried. Now, as the
lapse of many centuries had given time to his descendants by Ishmael's daughter to pervade the interior of Arabia under the name of Nabatheans [1],
may it not be useful to observe upon Ishmael's
blessing as well as upon Esau's, in order to see
whether, in the leading features of each, we may
not find prototypes of some of the great events
which originated in Arabia? These, we have
stated in the beginning of this chapter, have never
hitherto been recognised as fulfilments of the intimations in Esau's blessing, because it was never
considered that he was virtually in that country,
while in vain did commentators search in Ishmael's
blessing for hints of the *great dominion*, which,
under the Saracens, so notoriously spread from
Arabia.

---

[1] "The Saracens, or Nabatheans, possessed that part of Arabia
Felix bordering upon Arabia Petræa and Arabia Deserta; but
what was the extent of this territory we are not informed."
Universal History, vol. xvi. p. 255.

"The Cophtonim and Khorites, occupying the hilly district
about Mount Seir, though very ancient, never made any consider-
able figure. The posterity of Edom, who, after their excision,
seized upon the tract they inhabited, in process of time intermix-
ing with the proper Arabs, formed one people with them; but
neither do the present Arabs esteem Esau or Edom as one of the
real founders of their nation." Universal Hist. vol. xvi. p. 266.

It is elsewhere observed that the Arraceni and Saraceni of the
ancients were the same people.

Ishmael's blessing denotes him to be an *archer*, a robber, a wild man; and it intimates that his descendants will become a great nation. His twelve princes, however, indicate only petty chiefs; and such a sort of government (exclusive of the great dominion of the Saracens,) has always prevailed in Arabia. This brings us to examine Esau's blessing, he being another Patriarch of the same country. "*By thy* SWORD *shalt thou live.*" In the first instance Esau acquired the mountains of Seir by the sword; and his descendants, as Idumæans, were decidedly of a military character, and served the Israelites as auxiliary troops. So far, however, were they, in their character of Idumæans, from breaking Jacob's yoke from off their necks, that, in the time of David, king of Israel; "He put garrisons in Edom: throughout all Edom put he garrisons: and all they of Edom became David's servants." (2 Sam. viii. 14.) This was certainly a fulfilment of the prophecy that Esau should serve his brother, but, in the course of time, the posterity of Esau ceased to be the mark of observation, and their very name, as before mentioned from Bishop Newton, was forgotten in the second century. Even the site of their ancient capital, Petra, was not known for some hundred years, till that long deserted scene of rocks and sepulchres was discovered by Burkhardt, in his travels through Syria, a few years since. But, although thus forgotten by the world, we must not for one moment conceive that the posterity of such a subject of prophetic delineation as Esau, described so remarkably in the thirty-sixth chapter of Genesis, can really become extinct in all his three branches before the *last* days. In his blessing also he is at some period to have a dominion. This must be a dominion of notoriety, or it would not have been predicted. It is true that involvement in other tribes, migration, or change of denomination, may have obscured the three departments of his race, but dominion having been promised to him, it must rise up somewhere in his lineage.

The Jewish Rabbis trace *Edom* to Rome, and ancient history shows that a colony of Itureans came from the earliest times, and settled in Italy. The greater prophets have shown that *red Edom* is to be in action in the last days. And, as the three marked branches of *red Esau's* descendants can (according to the permission which the *red* horses of Zechariah obtained,) "walk to and fro through the earth[1]", we may still look for some

---

[1] "And the bay went forth, and sought to go that they might walk to and fro through the earth: and he said, Get you hence, walk to and fro through the earth. So they walked to and fro through the earth. Chap. vi. 7.

In the book of Job, and in a scene certainly passing upon the earth, Satan appears before the Lord, and, upon being questioned, answers, "that he had been walking to and fro in the earth."

further discovery of their occasionally different
positions upon earth, according to the promise that
" Esau shall be made so bare that he shall not be
able to hide himself." Having stated that the
learned Jewish Rabbis have expressed their belief
that there is a mystic connection between Rome and
Edom, it may be added that some human probabili-
ties are to be found in Brydone [1], that a grandson of

[1] "Next to Chamaseno, Palermo is generally supposed to be the
most ancient city in Sicily. Indeed there still remain some monuments that carry its origin to the times of the most remote antiquity. A bishop of Lucera has wrote on this subject. He is
clearly of opinion that Palermo was founded in the days of the
first patriarchs. You will laugh at this ;—so do I :—but the
bishop does not go to work upon conjecture only : he supports his
opinion with such proofs as I own to you staggered me a good
deal. A Chaldean inscription was discovered about six hundred
years ago on a block of white marble. It was in the reign of
William II., who ordered it to be translated into Latin and
Italian. The bishop says there are many fragments in Palermo,
with broken inscriptions in this language, and seems to think it
beyond a doubt that the city was founded by the Chaldeans in
the very early ages of the world. This is the literal translation :—' During the time that Isaac, the son of Abraham,
reigned in the valley of Damascus, and Esau, the son of Isaac, in
Idumea, a great number of Hebrews, accompanied by many of
the people of Damascus, and many Phœnicians, coming into this
triangular island, took up their habitation in this most beautiful
place, to which they gave the name of Panormus.' " Brydone,
vol. ii. p. 263.

" The bishop translated another Chaldean inscription, which is
indeed a great curiosity. It is still preserved, though not with
that care that so valuable a monument of antiquity deserves. It

Esau and a colony of Chaldeans *did* settle in Sicily. Our first pursuit, however, must be after that division, which appeared to spring up in Arabia, under the *name* of *Saracens.* For no

is placed over one of the old gates of the city, and when that gate falls to ruin, it will probably be for ever lost. The translation is in Latin, but I shall give it you in English :—' There is no other God but one God. There is no other power but this same God. There is no other conqueror but this God whom we adore. The commander of this Tower is Saphu, the son of Eliphaz, son of Esau, brother of Jacob, son of Isaac, son of Abraham. The name of the tower is Baych, and the name of the neighbouring tower is Pharat.'

" These two inscriptions seem to reflect a mutual light upon each other. Fazzelo has preserved them both, and remarks upon this last that it appears evidently from it, that the tower of Baych was built antecedent, to the time of Saphu, (or as he translates it, Zephu), who is only mentioned as commander of the Tower, but not as its founder. Part of the ruins of this tower still remain and many Chaldean inscriptions have been found among them.... Conversing on this subject the other night with a gentleman who is well versed in the antiquities of this place, he assured me, in respect to the original name given to Palermo, that Pan-ormus or something very nearly of the same sound, signified in the Chaldean language, and likewise in the Hebrew, a paradise, or delicious garden. He added too, that Panormus was likewise an Arabic word, and signified *this water;* which probably was the reason that the Saracens did not change its name, as they have done that of almost every thing else ; as this is as applicable, and as expressive of the situation of Palermo, as any of the other ety- mologies ; it being surrounded on all sides with beautiful fountains of the purest water, the natural consequence of the vicinity of the mountains."—*Brydone,* vol. ii. p. 264.

sooner had Esau's descendants ceased to be noted by their own name in Idumæa, than there was seen rising in the adjoining land, (a country marked out by Scripture, as the original station of Ishmael's and Esau's posterity), a religious power at once *warlike, profane,* and *persecuting,* the three branding marks of Ishmael and Esau. And this power became a great *dominion,* the very fulfilment we have been taught to look for in Esau's blessing. Still it must eventually be a transitory dominion, because the prime blessing of Isaac had made Jacob lord over him; and the words, as they run, denote that the dominion was an adventitious circumstance. "*It shall come to pass, that* WHEN *thou shalt have the dominion, his yoke shall pass from off thy neck.*" It is well known to history, that, during the destructive tyranny of the Romans in the first century, and the subsequent dominion of the Saracens in the seventh, there was no yoke of the Jews left upon any of the inhabitants of Idumæa or Arabia. King David's people no longer *had garrisons throughout all Edom.* The yoke had passed away.

But, to return to Ishmael and Esau. They had both been excluded from the heavenly inheritance, the one by Sarah's approved denunciation, and the other by the sale of his birthright, and also by the loss of his blessing on the authority of *his* mother, Rebekah, an authority certainly sanctioned to our apprehension by the example of Sarah's approved authority over the succession of *her* son. These two Arabian patriarchs, Ishmael and Esau, were therefore both inimical to the true inheritors. Ishmael was shown to be *mocking* from the first, and is in the New Testament said to be a *persecutor* of those born of the *promise*. (Galatians, iv. 29.)

And Esau (Genesis xxvii. 41.) hated his brother Jacob, and purposed in his heart to slay him at some distant period. But as neither Ishmael nor Esau appear to have hurt either Isaac or Jacob, during the term of their own natural lives, it is in the future deeds of their disappointed progeny that we must look for the fulfilment of their *persecution* and *hatred*. Accordingly, in the sixth century, by means of the forgeries of the self-constituted prophet of Arabia, " the tabernacles of Edom, and the Ishmaelites" (Psalm lxxxiii.) were enabled, sword in hand, to deny, in part, the authenticity of God's ancient covenant with his chosen people the Jews ; and also, in part, that of the new covenant of his Son with the Christians. Assuming to themselves the superiority, and thus claiming to be the *true heritors*, they endeavoured to set aside both the Old and the New Testament of God, and the blessings of Abraham and Isaac, their natural fathers, and enforced their pretensions with the *sword* and *persecution* from the very beginning.

Gibbon speaks of the implacable *hatred* of Mahomet against the Jews, and of the consequent *persecution* which he instituted against them ; and it is surely remarkable that this talented but sceptical historian should have used, upon this occasion, the very term by which the New Testament designates the conduct of Ishmael, in the epistle to the Galatians,—
" *But as then he that was born after the flesh,* PERSECUTED *him that was born after the spirit, even so it is now.*"

In the Old Testament, Ishmael's descendants are marked as *archers*, and, in Jacob's blessing to Joseph, he says, at the 23rd verse, " The ARCHERS have sorely grieved him, and shot at him, and hated him." The records of history show how truly this was fulfilled by the Saracens upon the Jews. But if we only consider one terrific instance, mentioned by Gibbon, which will be more fully stated hereafter, of seven hundred true Israelites having been burnt alive by Mahomet, because they would not desert their fathers' covenant, are we not, according to the purpose of remote fulfilments, unavoidably reminded of the *old hatred,* and the purpose of Esau to slay Jacob when his father should be dead ?   In fact, did not Esau's continued hatred break out when his progeny got the dominion hinted at in his blessing ? Was not that blessing apparently fulfilled by the Saracen's *dominion?* And is not the *persecuting* spirit evinced to this day,

G

in the disdainful behaviour of every Mahometan to
both Jews and Christians ?   The common term for
the latter is Christian dog.

If, upon research, it is found to be probable, that
the martial spirit of Esau, operating in the Naba-
thæan division of his descendants, was the spring of
that warlike disposition which suddenly arose in
Arabia, and produced the Saracenic conquests in
the seventh and eighth centuries, shall we not see
the fulfilment of the *sword*, and the dominion, given
to Esau in Isaac's blessing, some thousand years
before ? For by contrasting the two blessings, we
find that Esau has a *sword* but no *wine*, and Jacob
has *wine* but no *sword*; in accordance with which,
at *this* day, the Israelites have decidedly *no sword*,
and the Mahometans have *no wine*, being by fundamental law prohibited from using it.   And, surely,
that remarkable prohibition of wine in the Mahometan code, if we proceed under the apprehension,
that Esau was incorporated in Arabia, will clearly
show his necessary obedience to the original mandate of Isaac; who, after telling him that he had
made Jacob lord over him, proceeds to say, that he
had also sustained Jacob with corn and wine ; and
as if this comprised all that was most essential,
adds pathetically, " And what can I do now unto
thee, my son ?" The corn and wine therefore,
as far as concerns the mode in whtch Isaac meant
to confer them, are really given *away* from Esau ;

and we must conclude that his posterity cannot be sustained by them in the same *especial* manner in which Jacob's posterity can[1]; and that corn and wine were bestowed upon Jacob's posterity, in an especial, or *mystic* manner, is evident from the certainty, that the *dew* of *heaven*, and the *fatness* of the earth, which Isaac had conferred upon both the brothers alike, would in a *common* way afford it to each.

We have then to seek, among the remote fulfilments, for some statements which may show, that Isaac's blessing did eventually confer the corn and wine in an especial, or exclusive manner, upon Jacob's posterity.

It is distinctly shown in Scripture, that Ishmael was born of the flesh; and *as* distinctly that Esau was obnoxious to God. He, therefore, could not be the promised seed, which *was to be born of Isaac*. Jacob then must either be the promised seed himself, or one spiritually born, from whom the promised seed might descend; and one born of the Spirit can be spiritually sustained as well as bodily.

When, therefore we find, that, upon the miraculous deliverance of the posterity of Jacob from the bondage of Egypt, they were instructed and enjoined, by the Divine word, to commemorate for

---

[1] "Thou hast put joy and gladness in my heart, since the time that their corn, and wine, and oil increased."—*Psalm* iv. 8.

ever their escape, by the feast of unleavened bread
and the drink offering of wine ; do we not perceive
in that ordinance a remote fulfilment of the mystic
blessing of Isaac, when he exclusively endowed
Jacob's posterity with what he termed the *sustenance* of corn and wine ?   In fact, the ceremony of
taking them at the appointed times, has ever since
cemented that people together, and distinguished
them from all other nations, and no doubt mystically
sustains them.   " Thus saith the Lord God ; Although I have cast them far off among the heathen,
and although I have scattered them among the
countries, yet will I be to them as a little sanctuary
in the countries where they shall come." (Ezekiel
xi. 16) And, as if in continuation of that Divine
ordinance, when our Saviour, who was descended
in perfect generations from Isaac, dispensed a somewhat new covenant from the bosom of the old—he,
as if in lineal succession, ordained likewise a sacra-
mental memento like unto it, of bread and wine ;
by which we of the new covenant might also for
ever commemorate his glorious death, and our
deliverance thereby from the bondage of Satan. It
is true, that the new covenant is as yet more generally accepted by Gentiles than by Jews, but it
still holds the purport of Isaac's blessing to Jacob,
in the elements of bread and wine. When the
fulness of the Gentiles is come in, and the blindness
of the Jews removed, they will, upon accepting the
new covenant, and taking the Lord's supper, per-

ceive that it is but a slightly varied continuation of their own feast of unleavened bread, and the drink offering of wine; in which, by the way, there is probably that *hidden manna* promised to him that overcometh, that is, to him that receiveth worthily.

But THIS bread and wine the Mahometan *cannot* taste, or be *sustained* by, having renounced all allegiance to either of the covenants of the revealed God of Abraham. The Mahometan, therefore, cannot be nourished, or sustained, by those ordinances which conferred the *predicted corn* and *wine* upon Jacob. And thus do the posterities of Ishmael and Esau remain beyond the pale of the inheritance, which Sarah originally declared that Ishmael should do, and which inheritance Rebekah afterwards prevented Esau from obtaining: while we of the new covenant, instructed by our Lord himself, pray daily for *bread,* according to the information given to us in St. John, chap. vi.

Ver. 32. " Then Jesus said unto them, Verily, verily, I say unto you, Moses gave you not that bread from heaven, but my Father giveth you the true bread from heaven.

Ver. 33. "For the bread of God is he which cometh down from heaven, and giveth life unto the world.

Ver. 34. "Then said they unto him, Lord, evermore give us this bread."

It has been already suggested, that, in Isaac's much prized blessing of corn, we may perhaps include the hidden *manna* more openly promised in the New Testament to *him that overcometh*. The overcoming of evil is a task proposed to us, for our benefit, from the beginning of Scripture to the end; nothing, therefore, but gross self-deception, can keep us either ignorant, or slothful, or indifferent to the blessed victory, which we may obtain if we choose to strive for it.

The whole chapter of Obadiah treats upon the subject of *Edom* and his *confederacy*, describing it apparently in the different stages of its course. First, in the 2nd verse, as thus: " Behold, I have made thee small among the heathen; thou art greatly despised." Then, in the 3rd verse, giving intimations of a dominion, which, " the Lord will bring down;" adding, at the 6th verse, the following corroboration of Jeremiah's information, concerning the future discoveries to be made with respect to Esau, " How are the things of Esau searched out! how are his hidden things sought up!" And the last verse of this explicit chapter says, " And saviours shall come up on Mount Zion to judge the mount of Esau; and the kingdom shall be the Lord's!"

The 14th verse of the thirty-fifth chapter of Ezekiel, also, when addressing Mount Seir, apparently alludes to the end of the world, as thus: " When the whole earth rejoiceth, I will make thee desolate." There are many other passages in the Old Testament to the same purport; and the New Testament declares in confirmation that a man of sin will be revealed in the last days. " Let no man deceive you by any means ; for that day shall not come, except there come a falling away first, and that man of sin be revealed, the son of perdition."

This revealing seems to answer to the previous declaration in the Old Testament, where it is said, that *Esau shall be made so bare, that he shall not be able to hide himself*. And all doubt of his identity as Edom is, as before mentioned, provided against in the thirty-sixth chapter of Genesis.

[1] 2 Thess. ii. 3.

CHAPTER IV.

TWELFTH OF REVELATIONS.

"I always read the Scriptures," said an aged and pious divine, "as if they were a new book, and I had never read them in my life before,—as a book by which I am one day to be tried."

IT has already been remarked, in a note at the commencement of the chapter on the Metallic Image, that the Revelation of St. John appears to relate the subjects of a prophetic book, which was opened in the fifth chapter, while, at the 10th verse of the last chapter, St. John is informed that the sayings of the prophecy of this book were *not* to be sealed, because the time was at hand. We have seen, on the contrary, that when Daniel wrote five hundred years before St. John's time, he was expressly told that *his* prophecies were *shut up and sealed* till the *time of the end.* Now we are at present entering upon a series of prophecy written in the year of our Lord 96; and his atoning death is often adverted to as having taken place. We are therefore clearly in the Christian period, or *time of the end,* when the words of Daniel may begin to be

unclosed.   Commentators, indeed, have already
observed, that, upon the opening of the seals, there
issues from some of them a chronological series of
events reaching from the beginning of the Christian
æra to the end of the world.   The venturous endeavour therefore must still be, to see how far
their abstruse relations synchronize with, or in any
degree illustrate, those latter parts of the more
concise prophecies of the Old Testament, which
appear to be prototypes.

The brief remarks, which were made in the
second chapter, upon the dark and heathen times
of Daniel's predicted empires, joined to the corroborations of profane history, cannot fail to convince
us that those empires were, from the first commencement of the new world till the dawn of
Christianity, without any authorized knowledge of
God.   Now, when we remember that Noah, a
preacher of righteousness, was God's agent to conduct the selected remnant of the human race from
the ark, the widely extended apostasy, which succeeded the Deluge, argues of itself that there must
have been *active rebellion*, and that the spirit of
men, specifically so called, *still strove against God*.
It is true that Shem, of the blessed God, was
among them ; but Satan reigned for his permitted
and avowed term, and Shem either could not, or
was not intended to, be distinguished under such a
cloud.

The first city that was founded was by Nimrod,

whose name signifies *rebellion*. In the mean time, the whole Israel of God were in bondage. None of these things however are unnoted by Scripture. Thus in Isaiah lx. 2, we read,—"*For behold the darkness shall cover the earth, and gross darkness the people: but the Lord shall arise upon thee, and his glory shall be seen upon thee.*" The complaints of the long-suffering community of God's people are abundantly perceptible in the Psalms ; and the eighty-ninth Psalm appears to relate the terms of the covenant originally made by the Deity with his servant David (figuring the Messiah) concerning his community of people or children; and apparently the surname of Israel was given to Jacob, that the general community of Christ's people might occasionally be alluded to under that appellation, in contradistinction to the deceived adherents of Satan, who are often alluded to as *men*. The *exclusive* sons of Adam, oppressed by Satan's long predominance, may be found to utter their penitence, their supplications, their overwhelming sorrows, and their abhorrence of the enemies of God, in some of the following Psalms ; and many more might be adduced. " O God, how long shall the adversary reproach ? shall the enemy blaspheme thy name for ever ?" Psalm lxxiv. 10. " Why withdrawest thou thy hand, even thy right hand ? pluck it out of thy bosom." 11th verse. (In the translation in the Book of Common Prayer, " *why pluckest thou not thy right hand out of thy bosom to*

consume the enemy ?") In the 1st verse of the
fifty-seventh Psalm, " Be merciful unto me, O God,
be merciful unto me : for my soul trusteth in thee :
yea, in the shadow of thy wings will I make
my refuge, until these calamities be overpast"
(" until this *tyranny be overpast ;*" Prayer Book
Translation). In Psalm xviii. 27, 28. " For thou
wilt save the afflicted people ; but wilt bring down
high looks" (" the high looks of the proud:"
Common Prayer). " For thou wilt *light my candle*,
the Lord my God will enlighten my darkness"
(" *make my darkness to be light*" Common Prayer.)
This was the foreseen light of the Gospel. So
Isaiah, in the 1st and 2nd verses of his fortieth
chapter, " Comfort ye, comfort ye my people, saith
your God. Speak ye comfortably to Jerusalem,
and cry unto her, that her warfare is accomplished,
that her iniquity is pardoned." And again, in the
1st verse of the sixtieth chapter, " Arise, shine, for
thy light is come, and the glory of the Lord is
risen upon thee." And once more, in the 9th
verse of the twenty-fifth chapter, " And it shall
be said in that day, Lo, this is our God ; we have
waited for him, and he will save us : this is the
Lord ; we have waited for him, we will be glad and
rejoice in his salvation."

We may therefore now resort to the New Testament for some elucidations concerning the beginning of this promised emancipation.

REVELATIONS, CHAP. XII.

Ver. 1. " And there appeared a great wonder in heaven; a woman clothed with the sun, and the moon under her feet, and upon her head a crown of twelve stars :

Ver. 2. " And she, being with child, cried, travailing in birth, and pained to be delivered.

Ver. 3. " And there appeared another wonder in heaven; and behold a great red dragon, having seven heads and ten horns, and seven crowns upon his heads.

Ver. 4. " And his tail drew the third part of the stars of heaven, and did cast them to the earth : and the dragon stood before the woman which was ready to be delivered, for to devour her child as soon as it was born.

Ver. 5. " And she brought forth a man child, who was to rule all nations with a rod of iron : and her child was caught up unto God, and to his throne.

Ver. 6. " And the woman fled into the wilderness, where she hath a place prepared of God, that they should feed her there a thousand, two hundred and threescore days.

Ver. 7. " And there was war in heaven : Michael and his angels fought against the dragon; and the dragon fought and his angels,

Ver. 8. " And prevailed not; neither was their place found any more in heaven.

Ver. 9. " And the great dragon was cast out, that old serpent, called the Devil, and Satan, which deceiveth the whole world : he was cast out into the earth, and his angels were cast out with him.

Ver. 10. " And I heard a loud voice saying in heaven, Now is come salvation, and strength, and the kingdom of our God, and the power of his Christ : for the accuser of our brethren is cast down, which accused them before our God day and night.

Ver. 11. " And they overcame him by the blood of the Lamb, and by the word of their testimony ; and they loved not their lives unto the death.

Ver. 12. " Therefore rejoice, ye heavens, and ye that dwell in them, Woe to the inhabiters of the earth, and of the sea ! for the devil is come down unto you, having great wrath, because he knoweth that he hath but a short time.

Ver. 13. " And when the dragon saw that he was cast unto the earth, he persecuted the woman which brought forth the man *child.*

Ver. 14. " And to the woman were given two wings of a great eagle, that she might fly into the wilderness, into her place, where she is nourished for a time, and times, and half a time, from the face of the serpent.

Ver. 15. " And the serpent cast out of his mouth water as a flood after the woman, that he might cause her to be carried away of the flood.

Ver. 16. " And the earth helped the woman, and the earth opened her mouth, and swallowed up the flood which the dragon cast out of his mouth.

Ver. 17. " And the dragon was wroth with the woman, and went to make war with the remnant of her seed, which keep the commandments of God, and have the testimony of Jesus Christ."

This chapter is evidently the beginning of a subject, and it was written in the first century of the Christian æra. It may therefore appropriately narrate and symbolize the birth of Christianity, with the well-known perils and flight of the mother church, to whose tribulations an epoch is thus given. There being, however, two sections in this chapter, the first relating a scene passing in heaven and the second one passing upon the earth, we must be aware that either different periods or different stations may be meant. In the first, we have, as was seen in the beginning of the world, a manifest and terrific portrait of an evil spirit, which is known to be the old serpent of the third of Genesis, by his continued enmity to the woman, and her seed, the church. The subject of this chapter is therefore evidently a link of the same chain which began with the history of the fall. And as this scene is marked as passing in heaven, it may be an allegorical representation of that dissent, and consequent war, described in the 7th verse, which we may suppose consecutively to have taken place, when Satan foresaw that the birth of Christ upon earth would be the means of promulgating that efficient religion, which was calculated to destroy his works, and the *dominion* which he claimed in the world, and which he had enjoyed all through the preceding empires from the time of Babylon. He and his angels would therefore certainly oppose such a birth; and, being vanquished, were cast out into the earth, where, it is added in the 12th verse, great *woe* will be the consequence *to the inhabiters* of the earth.

The second section, beginning at the 13th verse, appears to relate scenes which really pass upon the earth, but, the chief actor having been designated in heaven by certain attributes, we know the station from which he acted in the world. The great woe, foretold at the 12th verse, must be looked upon as fulfilled upon the Christian Church, by the persecutions emanating from the seven hills of Rome, that is, from the power of the dragon. We cannot indeed account for those inhuman persecutions upon any other principle, because the Roman government was lenient to every other form of religion. This of itself indicates that there was an antichristian spirit within it. Even the acute Mr. Gibbon is at a loss to account upon common principles for the great and sanguinary violence of the Roman government against the primitive Christians, to the purity and sufferings of whom he bears ample testimony. And when, in the second chapter of the Revelations, and at the 10th verse, the church is warned of its troubles for *ten days*, (the ten persecutions,) can we fail to perceive the prescience of that statement, written as it was in the first century of the Christian æra?

We shall here transcribe a passage from the notes of the Pictorial Bible, on the thirty-sixth chapter of Genesis, 9th verse. The subject has been already alluded to in the chapter concerning Esau, but it seems desirable to state it more fully here.

"Perhaps we ought not to conclude this article, without noticing the belief entertained by the Jews and Mohammedans, that the original Romans were a colony of Edomites. Their accounts somewhat differ as to times and persons, but they agree in substance; and are all doubtless derived from the same source—the teaching of the Rabbins. Hence the Jews apply to Rome whatever the prophets say of the destruction of Edom in the latter times. The Talmud calls Italy and Rome 'the cruel empire of Edom.' The Mohammedans consider that both the Greeks and Latins are descended from Roum, the son of Esau; but it does not appear from the chapter before us, that Esau had any such son."

H

There is in Brydone [1] an account of an inscription upon a marble block, dug up among the ruins of a fort in Messina, stating that Eliphaz, son of Esau, Jacob's brother, commanded that fort. According to Brydone, an Italian Bishop has written a pamphlet upon the subject. It is found likewise in the Ancient History, vol. ii. p. 242, that the Umbrians were one of those early colonies which first came to Italy out of Asia; and, at page 252, that the language used in Umbria and Etruria, savoured of the remotest antiquity, most of the Tuscan words being of oriental extraction. Now, it has been shown, in the preceding chapter, that Esau is as strongly marked in prophecy as Jacob. He is four times marked to be *Edom*, as we have seen, in one chapter, the thirty-sixth of Genesis. Now, *red Edom* is, from the first book of the Old Testament to the last, a beacon name for a division of the Antichristian power, which is to pervade this world to the end of it. We have seen it recorded that Esau married three wives, but all of them were without the pale of the chosen race, and of his posterity the most inwrapt prophecies were delivered a thousand years after his personal appearance upon earth. Isaac's pregnant blessing to him was, "*By thy sword thou shalt live.*" If then, in Italy, one of *red* Esau's three branches did take root, it would naturally follow

[1] See the note in the preceding chapter, p. 77.

that they would rise up *swordsmen.* The mystery
of Esau's important history, having been already
considered, need not be introduced here, but the
learned Jewish Rabbins, having perceived that there
is a secret connection between Rome and *Edom,*
we cannot but be greatly struck by the portrait of
the dragon, here characteristically marked by the
red colour, and the *seven hills* of Rome, in a book of
prophecy which the Jews never read.

To the rider of the *red* horse in the second seal,
(Rev. vi. 4.) a great *sword* was given, and it was
allowed him to take peace from the earth. This
corresponds with the great *woe* foretold at the
twelfth verse, and still keeps in view the mystic
colour and the warlike disposition of Esau's
progeny. It may therefore here be useful to
advert to the symbolic horses of Zechariah, which
will be more fully treated of in future. It is found,
in the 7th verse of the sixth chapter, that the
bay (or *red*) horses sought, and had reluctant leave,
to walk *to* and *fro* through the earth, so that
their power was not to be stationary; and according to this liberty given to the *red* horses, we shall
find that the *red* dragon gives his power, and his
seat, unto a beast like unto a leopard in the next
chapter.

Ver. 17. "And the dragon was wroth with the
woman, and went to make war with the remnant
of her seed, which keep the commandments of
God, and have the testimony of Jesus Christ."

The dragon therefore will make war, both upon those who keep the commandments of God, the Jews; and also upon those who have the testimony of Jesus Christ, that is, the Christians. According to this prediction, the Roman power first destroyed Jerusalem in the year 70, and then proceeded with the endeavour to extirpate the "*bleeding remnant*" of the Christian Church. And, for the *enmity* of such a *device*, we may see a further cause in the New Testament. In the fourth chapter of Luke we find that our Lord was tempted of Satan, and our excellent Bishop Porteus has, in his lectures, given it as his opinion, that the transaction passed literally upon this earth, as we know that our Lord was literally upon it at the time, "And the Devil said unto him, If thou be the Son of God, command this stone that it be made bread." (Ver. 3.)— "And he brought him to Jerusalem, and set him on a pinnacle of the temple, and said unto him, If thou be the son of God, cast thyself down from hence." (Ver. 9.)—Now, although it would not perhaps be justifiable to deduce from these two verses that Satan was not quite certain of the identity of Christ, yet the supposition of the fact would harmonize with several other parts of Scripture, where secrecy is enjoined, and mystery acknowledged to exist, till after the crucifixion, by which our redemption was ensured, had taken place. Our Saviour frequently desires secrecy; and admitting that there were two communities of people in

Jerusalem, the one being perfect in their generations, and the other contaminated by their inter-
mixture with the forbidden Canaanitish nations,
we must see the reason for a discriminating disclo-
sure concerning the mission and person of Christ.
The intimation of his Advent upon earth had been
so deeply inwrapt in the Old Testament, and
further so closely inshrined by the long course of
four thousand years, that Satan himself might have
been kept in doubt about the exact time of his
appearance ; and this might have been ordered by
the wise counsels of God, lest *he*, whose extreme
subtilty had effected the fall of man, should again
interfere to obstruct his redemption. Thus St.
Paul says, (1 Cor. ii. 7, 8.) "We speak the
wisdom of God *in a mystery*, even the *hidden
wisdom*, which God ordained before the world unto
our glory : which *none* of the *princes of this world
knew :* for *had they known it,* they *would not have
crucified the Lord of glory."*

Caiaphas the high priest was so anxious about
the identity of our Saviour, that he says, (Mat.
xxvi. 63.) "*I adjure thee by the living God, that
thou tell us whether thou be the Christ, the Son
of God."* In harmony with the view here taken,
we find that the answer to questioners was sometimes clear, and at other times perfectly evasive.
The division of the people also, in point of opinion,
concerning the identity of our Lord, is often mentioned in the Gospels. Still Jesus Christ had said

" *My sheep know my voice,*" and this was sufficient
for the purpose of calling those to whom he chose
to disclose himself.   His humble station in life
indicates that he meant only to be partially known
till the crucifixion had taken place.

(Luke iv. 8.) " And Jesus answered and said
unto him, Get thee behind me, Satan : for it is
written, Thou shalt worship the Lord thy God,
and him only shalt thou serve."

From all this we are permitted to see plainly
that Satan was in an active state of rebellion
against God ; and desirous to gain the acquiescence
of our Lord in his pretensions, as well as to induce
him to fall down and worship him.   We are not
indeed given to understand the previous circumstances of the case, but when Satan asserts that
the dominion of this world had been delivered to
him, and when our Lord does not deny the statement, but afterwards styles him Prince of this
world, we certainly receive positive information of
that fact, and it is in accordance with many other
passages in Scripture.   Jesus, however, having
utterly rejected the proffered temptation, it is
obvious, that the dominion remained in Satan's
possession.   Having therefore such power and
strength in his hands, it was to be expected that a
disappointed spirit, rebellious, subtile, and ambitious, would resort to some *device*, some mighty
scheme, by which to lower our Saviour, and still to
arrogate worship to himself.   In the seventh cen-

tury, consequently, when Paganism began to fail before the Gospel, the wonderful project of Mahometanism arose, and was evidently calculated, first to degrade the Saviour, and then to exterminate Christianity. The pretence indeed 'was to abolish idolatry, but, had that been the really pious intent, the religion of the Jews would have been all sufficient; but they also were required to adulterate their ancient covenant with the revealed God, which proves that the author of the system in question was Satan, in a state of rebellion against him. Thus the opening of the bottomless pit, in the ninth of Revelations, under the first woe trumpet, appears to describe that disgorgement of Satanic agents, which commentators generally recognise as the prefiguration of the Saracenic irruptions in the seventh century, when the blasphemy of the Mahometan forgery was enforced at the point of the sword. And this still fulfils the great *woe* foretold at the 12th verse of this chapter, as all history can testify, while the self-styled scourgers of idolatry were flourishing in the glory of a great empire. The fact is that no extensive scheme of deception can gain credit sufficient to establish itself, without the plausible assumption of some virtue to assist it. Mahomet's personal inplacability against the Jews proved that idolatry was not his real aim. If retrospect may be here allowed, it was much more like Esau's long previous intention to slay his brother Jacob, the

promised seed, when opportunity should occur,
for there was no idolatry to act against in the Jews.
And, in stating the probability that *enmity* was the
cause of Mahomet's hatred against them, we would
refer to the preceding chapter, in which the circumstance has been stated of Esau's having married a daughter of Ishmael, and thereby spreading
a division of his descendants into Arabia.

Of the hatred of the Mahometans against the
Jews, there is ample proof in history. Mr. Gibbon,
having mentioned the refusal of the Jews to become
Mahometans, adds,—" Their obstinacy converted
his (Mahomet's) friendship into implacable hatred,
with which he pursued that unfortunate people to
the last moment of his life : and, in the double
character of an apostle and a conqueror, his persecution was extended to both worlds." Among
various instances of that persecution, Gibbon gives
the following :—" Seven hundred Jews were drag-
ged in chains to the market-place of the city;
where they *descended alive into the grave* prepared
for their execution and burial; and Mahomet
beheld with an inflexible eye the slaughter of his
hapless enemies[1]."

Had Mahomet been merely a well-meaning
enthusiast acting against idolatry, he would have
honoured the Jews, because they acknowledge
God alone. But surely the very reverse of this is
the case, and a preternatural *strength, enmity,* and

[1] Gibbon, vol. ix. p. 304.

antichristian spirit, is discernible in the whole procedure and success of such a plain forgery as the Mahometan religion exhibits, and particularly when considered with reference to Mahomet's disposition to slaughter the Jews.

Some of the chapters of this book (the Revelations) are evidently marked by a system of chronological order, and, as they draw towards the end, relate in succession, (although sometimes interspersed with other chapters,) the latter events of the world; but, as in this twelfth chapter there may be two successive stages of the Christian church related, so in the following thirteenth chapter there may be the portrait of a new power, which arose during the second stage of it, and which was also subsequent to the antichristian exertions of the Pagan Roman Empire, the Dragon, against the mother church. But the Dragon, it will be found, gives his power, and his strength, and great authority, to the *new* beast, of the next chapter; for if it is not a *new* beast, to whom did the dragon (always supposed to represent the Pagan Roman Empire) give his power and his strength? Did he give them to himself? No: that is contravened by the declining strength of the western empire, which entirely ceased in 476. But the empire of the Saracens arose in the next century, and the attributes of those two empires, when depicted in their universal states, are so much alike, that the one may be taken for the other, till history, chronology, and Scripture, united, shall decide upon the claim, which one of them certainly has, to fulfil the portrait of the fourth and last beast of Daniel's seventh chapter.

The Dragon, the Beast, and the false Prophet, are distinctly named in the sixteenth chapter, and that which comes from their mouths is said to be the spirits of devils ; and from circumstances, which are related, we may infer that these three antichristian powers sometimes act in conjunction and sometimes separately.   Nor is that supposition incompatible with the event of their occasionally acting against each other, whenever the special controul of an over-ruling Providence shall become necessary, as indeed is most clearly related in the seventeenth chapter.   That account, however, being given by one of the angels which pour out the *last plagues*, it must only be looked upon here as an anticipation, useful indeed to the present argument, but merely showing a future vision of the beast in his latter revived state, when the conflicts of the last times are to take place.   It gives us the consolation of seeing that, notwithstanding the acknowledged strength of the antichristian party, the balance which is finally to be turned against them is ever in the hand of God.   In fact, the like information concerning the restricted power of the antichristian party, during the process of our redemption under the great captain of our salvation, is discernible from the first chapter of Genesis to

the last of the Revelations.—(Revelations xii. 17.)
" And the dragon was wroth with the woman, and
went to make war with the remnant of her seed,
which keep the commandments of God, and have
the testimony of Jesus Christ."

The Jews keep the commandments of God, and
the Christians have the testimony of Jesus Christ.
It is therefore only a natural inference, that the
blasphemous beast of the next (thirteenth) chapter
is the mighty engine of war, which the deposed
dragon (Satan) went in his power to raise against
them, during his limited term of causing *woe upon
the earth,* according to the 12th verse of this
chapter.

REVELATIONS, CHAP. i.

Ver. 1. " The Revelation of Jesus Christ, which
God gave unto him, to show unto his servants
things which must shortly come to pass; and he
sent and signified it by his angel unto his servant
John :

Ver. 2. " Who bare record of the word of God,
and of the testimony of Jesus Christ, and of all
things that he saw.

Ver. 3. " Blessed is he that readeth, and they
that hear the words of this prophecy, and keep
those things which are written therein : for the
time is at hand."

" *For the time is at hand.*"   This surely indicates
that the events to be related in this book are future

events, that is future to the birth of Christianity.
The destruction of Jerusalem in the year 70, and the
ten persecutions, were the first sufferings of the Christian æra; and in the seventh century, the Mahometan
warriors entered upon the scene, with a rebellious
doctrine, enforced either at the point of the sword
or by crafty dealings. This again fulfils the *great
woe ;* and apparently continues the type of the man
riding a red horse, to whom a great sword had
been given, with power to take peace from the
earth. The *crafty dealings* were those terms of
apostacy, offered to the vanquished party, by which
they were compelled either to adopt the Mahometan religion or to pay grievous taxes, an infliction to which Christians are still subjected wherever
the Mahometan power has the ascendancy. This
woe, according to the information given in the
10th verse of the third chapter, was to *" come upon
all the world."* Now, the Mahometan temptation,
which *did come* in the seventh century, and was
spread over all the predicted part of the earth, is
well known to modern history. But an immature
prophecy is always liable to be mistaken for the
first object that happens to resemble it, and precedes the one really portrayed. This appears to
have been the case, when the Fathers of the
second and third centuries looked for the coming
of Antichrist as soon as the Roman Empire should
be taken out of the way, according to a very natural apprehension founded upon the second chap-

ter of the second epistle to the Thessalonians. Accordingly, after the fall of the western Roman Empire, the Pope became such an object of notice that, when a complete Antichrist subsequently arose in the person of Mahomet, he was comparatively little thought of as such. Yet no human creature ever so palpably, so openly, so undeniably, and so successfully, opposed himself to the revealed God and the Saviour, as Mahomet. And it will in due time appear that he is individually and plainly pointed out in prophecy. But the Scriptures were in part locked up, and the Apocalypse quite laid aside, so that, at the very time when some of the predictions contained in it were fulfilled, the world remained entirely ignorant of them. It ought perhaps here to be adverted to, that when, in the tenth chapter of that " *little book*," seven thunders uttered their voices, St. John was ordered to " *seal up those things which they uttered*." Yet, he is next informed, that, "in the days when the *seventh angel shall begin to sound, the mystery of God should be finished*." Moreover, after St. John had "eaten up the little book," which he received from the angel's hand, he was told that he must " prophesy *again* [1] before many peoples and nations

---

[1] Does not this clearly denote the latter elucidations of the Apocalypse? In the eleventh chapter of the Revelations, 1st and 2nd verses, we read as follows :—" And the angel stood, saying, Rise, and measure the temple of God, and the altar, and

and tongues." That "*again*" may therefore mean the *latter* elucidations and developments of the Apocalypse, which ignorance, intolerance, and the floating wit of the world, had hitherto concurred in keeping back. But, in the seventeenth century, the intrepid mind of Sir Isaac Newton pronounced that, when the Apocalypse should be rightly understood, it would prove a key to all the Ancient Scriptures.

Of those Scriptures the greatest mystery is the often mentioned Antichrist.

" The tyrannical power, described by Daniel and St. Paul, and afterwards by St. John, is, both by ancients and moderns, generally denominated Antichrist. The name began to prevail in St. John's time. (1 Epist. ii. 18. 22.) ' As ye have heard that Antichrist shall come, even now are there many Antichrists ; . . . . . Who is a liar but he that denieth that Jesus is the Christ ? He is Antichrist, that *denieth the Father and the Son.*' " (Is not this a plain description of Mahomet, and quite inapplicable to the Pope ?)

them that worship therein. But the court which is without the temple, leave out, and measure it not; for it is given unto the Gentiles : and the holy city shall they tread under foot forty and two months." Does not this, being a Christian prophecy, apparently describe that department of people, who worshipped the revealed God, and that department of people, who we know, did, and do, to this day, trample upon Jerusalem and the holy city of Christ's church,—the Mahometans ?

"Afterwards, (2 Epist. 7, 8.) he styleth him emphatically '*the deceiver and the Antichrist*,' and *warneth the Christians to ' look to themselves*.'

"The Fathers too speak of *Antichrist*, and of *the man of sin*, as one and the same person ; and give much the same interpretation that hath here been given of the whole passage : only it is not to be supposed that they, who wrote before the events, could be so very exact in the application of each particular, as those who have the advantage of writing after the events.

"Justin Martyr, who flourished before the middle of the second century, considers *the man of sin*, or, as he elsewhere calleth him, *the man of blasphemy*, as altogether the same with the little horn of Daniel.   Tertullian, who became famous at the latter end of the same century, expounding those words *only*, "he who now *letteth will let until he be taken out of the way*," says, who can this be but the Roman state ? . . . . . And, in his apology, he assigns it as a particular reason why the Christians prayed for the Roman Empire, because they knew that the greatest calamity hanging over the world was retarded by the continuance of it.

"Cyril of Jerusalem, in the same century, alleges this passage of St. Paul, together with other prophecies concerning Antichrist, and says that ' This the predicted Antichrist will come when the times of the Roman Empire shall be fulfilled.'   The comment upon St. Paul's epistle, which passeth

8

under the name of St. Ambrose, proposeth much the same interpretation, and affirms that after the failing of, or decay of, the Roman Empire, Antichrist shall appear.

"St. Chrysostom, in one of his homilies upon this passage, speaking of what hindered the revelation of Antichrist, asserts that ' when the Roman Empire shall be taken out of the way, then he shall come :' and it is very likely : for, as long as the dread of this Empire shall remain, no one will be quickly substituted ; but, when this shall be dissolved, he shall seize on the vacant Empire, and shall endeavour to assume the power both of God and man."

"In this manner," continues Bishop Newton, " these ancient and venerable Fathers expound this passage ; and in all probability, they had learned by tradition from the Apostles, or from the Church of the Thessalonians, that what retarded the revelation of Antichrist was the Pagan Roman Empire [1]."

If then we allow the Fathers, just quoted, to have obtained a certain and accurate perception of the great and mischievous power which was coming upon all the world, we must at the same time acknowledge that the Pope, who never denied Christ, could not so fully complete the character of the expected great Antichrist, as the Founder of the

[1] Bishop Newton on the Prophecies, vol. ii. p. 117.

Mahometan empire did in the seventh century. The fathers, however, had then ceased to exist, and the tyranny of the Pope having already shown itself at variance with the mild precepts of Christianity, he was by human opinion denominated the Antichrist. It is certain that two such momentous objects of prophetical announcement having been really manifested in the world, it will be necessary to keep our minds clear from confounding the two separate lines of prophecy which depict them; and whenever this discriminating attention fails, whether through indolence or misapprehension, we must remain with a more obscured view of the case, than the two representations, when fairly examined and accurately compared, would undoubtedly afford.

St. Paul's "man of sin" is a very direct prophecy, and he is not to be expected till after a falling away. Now, the most notable instance of falling away seems to have happened when the Eastern Empire pealed away from the Western, which so far weakened Rome, as to leave her subject to all the calamities which afterwards befel her, and made way, first, for an image of her former power in the Papal Supremacy, and secondly, for the Western conquests of the Saracens.

1

CHAPTER V.

THIRTEENTH OF REVELATIONS.

The thirteenth of Revelations, p. 115.—An Image of the former Roman tyranny rising in the Papistical head, p. 118.—An *approaching* dominion, so extraordinary as the Saracenic, more likely to be portrayed by St. John, as a *future* event, than either the past or present Roman empire, p. 119.—A portrait of the past or present of no service in the manifestation of prescience, p. 119.—That of the Saracenic empire of infinite service, p. 119.—Apparently, however, a reserved prophecy, and by what means, p. 119.—The universal beast of this chapter, like unto a leopard, his predecessor. The Saracenic empire spread nearly over the same ground, and possessed the same warlike character as the Roman, p. 120.—The seven heads of the Caliphate, p. 120.—Their blasphemous character, p. 120.—Transfer of the dragon's power to the blasphemous beast of this chapter, p. 121.—Probable advantage gained by Satan from Adam's fall, p. 122.—Our Saviour's rejection of his proffered temptation, p. 122.—Satan's disappointed ambition prompting him to give his power to some form of rebellion, acting particularly against the Saviour, p. 122.—The Saracenic such a power, p. 122.—The horses of Zechariah considered, p. 123.—The wounded head of the beast verified at Rome in the year 476, by the sword of the northern nations, and the preaching of the Gospel, p. 125.—Revives in the Papacy, p. 126.—The open enmity of the great beast of this chapter, p. 127.—Never fulfilled by the Roman power, but accurately verified by the Mahometan, p. 127.—The Churches of Rome and Constantinople, in spite of their

WE come now to the thirteenth chapter of the
Revelations, which we shall transcribe entire for
the convenience of the reader, preparatory to the
observations which we are about to make upon
its contents.

REVELATIONS, CHAP. xiii.

Ver. 1. "And I stood upon the sand of the sea,
and saw a beast rise up out of the sea, having
seven heads and ten horns, and upon his horns
ten crowns, and upon his heads, the name of blasphemy.

Ver. 2. "And the beast which I saw was like
unto a leopard, and his feet were as the feet of a
bear, and his mouth as the mouth of a lion: and
the dragon gave him his power, and his seat, and
great authority.

Ver. 3. "And I saw one of his heads as it were wounded to death; and his deadly wound was healed: and all the world wondered after the beast.

Ver. 4. "And they worshipped the dragon which gave power unto the beast: and they worshipped the beast: saying, Who is like unto the beast? who is able to make war with him?

Ver. 5. "And there was given unto him a mouth speaking great things and blasphemies; and power was given unto him to continue forty and two months.

Ver. 6. "And he opened his mouth in blasphemy against God, to blaspheme his name, and his tabernacle, and them that dwell in heaven.

Ver. 7. "And it was given unto him to make war with the saints, and to overcome them: and power was given him over all kindreds, and tongues, and nations.

Ver. 8. "And all that dwell upon the earth shall worship him, whose names are not written in the book of life of the Lamb slain from the foundation of the world.

Ver. 9. "If any man have an ear, let him hear.

Ver. 10. "He that leadeth into captivity shall go into captivity: he that killeth with the sword must be killed with the sword. Here is the patience and the faith of the saints.

Ver. 11. "And I beheld another beast coming up out of the earth; and he had two horns like a lamb, and he spake as a dragon.

Ver. 12. "And he exerciseth all the power of the first beast before him, and causeth the earth and them which dwell therein to worship the first beast, whose deadly wound was healed.

Ver. 13. "And he doeth great wonders, so that he maketh fire come down from heaven on the earth in the sight of men,

Ver. 14. "And deceiveth them that dwell on the earth by the means of those miracles which he had power to do in the sight of the beast; saying to them that dwell on the earth, that they should make an image to the beast, which had the wound by a sword, and did live.

Ver. 15. "And he had power to give life unto the image of the beast, that the image of the beast should both speak, and cause that as many as would not worship the image of the beast should be killed.

Ver. 16. "And he caused all, both small and great, rich and poor, free and bond, to receive a mark in their right hand, or in their foreheads.

Ver. 17. "And that no man might buy or sell, save he that had the mark, or the name of the beast, or the number of his name.

Ver. 18. "Here is wisdom. Let him that hath understanding count the number of the beast: for it is the number of a man; and his number is six hundred, threescore and six."

Not only at the opening of the Revelations, but, at the 1st verse of the fourth chapter, it is again said to St. John, "*I will shew thee things which must be* HEREAFTER."

At the time of St. John's beholding this vision, the Roman Empire was in a state of maturity, and the imperial rank allowed a crown to surmount the seven hills of Rome, nor did that mark of royalty cease till the Western Empire subsequently fell in 476. But *this rising* beast has seven heads *without* crowns, and one of them has a *deadly wound* by a *sword*, which proves to demonstration, that it is not one of the hills of Rome. If farther confirmation is necessary, this head is proved to be a proper beast's head, by the 14th verse of the chapter which we are now considering, which mentions "an image" raised "to the beast, which had the *wound* by a *sword*, and *did live*." And, after the fall of the Western Empire, and when the Latin tongue had become a dead language, there *did* arise in the papistical head an image of the former Roman tyranny as will be clearly shown.

In the meantime, however, we must first remark upon an exceedingly blasphemous empire, which, after the Western Empire fell (*or was taken out of the way*) began to arise in the seventh century, and spread all over the site of the Metallic

Image, and thereby became as competent to afford ten horns as the previous empire had been. Is it not then more reasonable to apprehend, that an *approaching* dominion, so extraordinary as the Saracenic turned out to be, would, according to the exordium of this book, be revealed or portrayed to St. John, as a *future* event, than that a useless portrait, either of the past or present Roman Empire, should be exhibited in the first century. A portrait of the past or present could be of no service in the manifestation of prescience ; whereas a true portrait given of the well known and entirely blasphemous empire of the Saracens, five hundred years before it appeared in the world, must be of infinite service to every one that could attain to a perception of its accuracy, by convincing them of the inspiration of Scripture. Apparently, however, it was a reserved prophecy, as many circumstances concurred to throw it into the shade. First, it so far resembled the Roman Empire, in those characteristics which were portrayed, as to be mistaken for it. Secondly, the Apocalypse itself, being immature, was, (and no doubt but by permission) laid aside for several centuries, as too abstruse and figurative to be understood.

Ver. 2. " *And the beast which I saw was like unto a leopard.*"—I have presumed that the Roman Empire was represented by a leopard in the seventh chapter of Daniel, and if that conjecture is right,

and if the dragon in the twelfth of the Apocalypse
represents the Pagan Roman Empire, it would
follow most naturally that the succeeding universal
beast of this chapter, which received the dragon's
dethroned power, and spread nearly all over the
same ground, should be in his body like unto a
leopard, his predecessor.   Likewise, having received the power and strength of the dragon, we
may consistently look for some of his attributes in
this beast, such as his ten horns; and the warlike
acquirements of the Saracenic Empire soon justified
such an expectation.

This beast has *seven* animated heads *without*
crowns, (the dragon *was* crowned,) and upon each
head the name of blasphemy.   After the rise of
the Saracenic Empire, which was *founded* in *blas-*
phemy, it was in 936 divided into seven heads or
kingdoms, as the chronological tables show.   And,
as long after as the eleventh century, when the
" Caliph Cayem appointed Togrol his temporal
vicegerent over the domains of Islamism, he was
presented with seven slaves, the natives of the
seven countries of the Empire of the Caliphs [1]."

The above mentioned seven heads, or official
portions of the dominion of the Saracens, were
surely as worthy of being recorded by prophecy
for their perfect blasphemy, as the seven hills of
Rome were, to characterise the station of the dragon.

---

[1] Mill's History of Mahommedanism, p. 288.

Ver. 2. "*And the dragon gave him his power, and his seat, and great authority.*"

This must in part be mystical, but we know that in general the Saracenic Empire, not only succeeded to the Roman, but occupied its territories. According to the early writers, both Jews and Christians, it has always been supposed that there was a Satanic Spirit in Rome; and the world has long since had visible and extensive proofs of it. Such are, first, the early persecution of the primitive Christians; secondly, the forcible introduction of images into their pure worship; thirdly, the strong and lasting endeavour to keep the Scriptures as secret as possible; and fourthly, the most cruel sacrifice of MILLIONS, who chose to understand those Scriptures plainly, and follow them in an obedient manner. This subject may, nevertheless, at first seem abstruse; yet, when we are told, in plain language, that the dragon gave his power to the combined, the Antichristian beast of this chapter, ought we to persist in being so far wise above what is written, as to doubt whether such a spiritual transfer can be made, and thereby forfeit the clew held forth for our information and guidance? Rather let our confidence in Scripture language lead us on in such a course of patient investigation, as may allow us to discern that it really was made by delegation.

The dragon was, in the twelfth chapter, shown to be cast upon the earth, and is without a doubt

Satan. In the fourth of Luke he offers the glory and the power of this world, (in which he appears to ·have reigned ever since the time of Babylon,) to our Saviour. Jesus Christ does not disallow that he had it to dispose of: and this tacit admission permits us to draw the conclusion, that Satan, although an evil, a vanquished, and a subordinate power, had gained some advantage in the rebellious war related in the twelfth chapter. And, if that advantage arose from Adam's fall, it was probably the temporary dominion of this world, which then, by right of conquest, fell into Satan's hands, and was, according to St. Luke, offered to our Lord as a temptation to gain his worship. Now, that offer being rejected, can we hesitate to believe, that Satan's disappointed ambition would prompt him to give that same power, and *dominion,* to some form of antichristian rebellion which might act *particularly* against the Saviour? In accordance with this, the Saracenic dominion *subsequently* shone out in great glory, and in undisguised enmity to our Lord Jesus Christ, apparently in strict agreement with the mention that the dragon gave his power, and his seat, to the antichristian beast of this chapter. There does also seem to be another remote fulfilment, in the circumstance of the head quarters of Mahometanism being now established in Constantinople, the last seat of the Roman emperors.

Before we enter more fully upon the subject

which now claims our attention, we ought perhaps to refer to the sixth of Zechariah, to which the attention of the reader has already been directed as a prototype chapter. It gives us information concerning four differently coloured horses. Now horses of a specific colour, with riders upon them, are one of the most important types of prophecy; and the angel, in this chapter of Zechariah, instructs us that the four horses here represent the *four spirits of the heavens, which go forth from standing before the Lord of all the earth.* The colour of *Red,* and that of *White,* Scripture has sufficiently notified as emblematic respectively of *good* and *evil.* The *Black* Horse in the sixth of the Apocalypse seems to denote the course of justice; while the *Grisled and Bay* of Zechariah, and the *Pale* Horse of the sixth of the Apocalypse appear to denote a latter commixture of the *Red* and the *White* previous to the great conflict of the last days. But our present inquiry is concerning the early going forth, and the local movements of Zechariah's specified horses. The bay, or *red,* sought to go, that they might walk to and fro through the earth, and had indignant leave.

ZECHARIAH, CHAP. vi. [1]

Ver. 1. "And I turned, and lifted up mine eyes,

[1] Job i. 6, 7. "Now there was a day when the sons of God came to present themselves before the Lord, and Satan came also

and looked, and, behold, there came four chariots out from between two mountains; and the mountains were mountains of brass.

Ver. 2. " In the first chariot were red horses; and in the second chariot black horses;

Ver. 3. " And in the third chariot white horses; and in the fourth chariot grisled and bay horses.

Ver. 4. " Then I answered and said unto the angel that talked with me, What are these, my lord ?

Ver. 5. " And the angel answered and said unto me, These are the four spirits of the heavens, which go forth from standing before the Lord of all the earth.

Ver. 6. " The black horses which are therein go forth into the north country; and the white go forth after them; and the grisled go forth toward the south country.

Ver. 7. " And the bay went forth, and sought to go that they might walk to and fro through the earth : and he said, Get you hence, walk to and fro through the earth. So they walked to and fro through the earth.

Ver. 8. " Then cried he upon me, and spake unto me, saying, Behold, these that go toward the north country have quieted my spirit in the north country."

---

among them. And the Lord said unto Satan, Whence comest thou? Then Satan answered the Lord, and said, From going to and fro in the earth, and from walking up and down in it."

The *spirit* of the Gospel has been more freely received, and better retained, in the northern countries than in any of the southern; we may therefore conjecture that some of the Aborigines of the North were the descendants of one of the approved sons of Noah, (according to geographers, Japhet,) and that, after the long season of gross darkness described by Isaiah in his sixtieth chapter, and fulfilled during the reign of Satan, these northern aborigines might be both more eligible, and more inclined, to receive the Gospel, than the southern descendants of Ham and Ishmael.   From *Shem*, in a midway station, the promulgation of the Gospel had been given; and the reception of it by Japhet's posterity, and the rejection of it by that of Ham, must be left to the tracings of history.   In the mean time, however, this transient allusion to the subject may not be thought inapplicable to our present purpose.

In the chapter of the Apocalypse, which we are now considering, we are told that one of the seven heads of the beast was wounded almost to death, but recovered and did live.

The Deity himself has foredoomed that enmity shall prevail, between the seed of the intellectual serpent, and the seed of the woman. This incidental information, given at the time of the fall, shows that there would henceforth be different seeds upon the earth; and that, owing to the ordained *enmity*, there would be continual warfare between them, and a mutual *bruising* on each part, to the end of the world. We therefore naturally look among the chronological prophecies for some farther notice of this preordained *bruising;* and upon some of the well known events of the world for its probable earthly fulfilment. Now here, in the New Testament, the elucidator of antecedent prophecy, we have the portrait of an eminent, and remarkably *bruised* head. It is represented as having been wounded by a sword; and, though it afterwards recovered, the *wound* nevertheless appears to constitute a *bruise* as much as the previous piercing of our Lord's *heel did.*

The head, we learn from the 14th verse of this chapter, was a proper beast's head, and upon this head was the name of blasphemy. It has already been observed that, either by tradition, or by the labour of commentators, Rome has always been considered as animated by Satan, *the serpent;* while that opinion has been confirmed by the violent operations of its spirit, first, against the people of the revealed God, and secondly, against the pure mode of worshipping him. It was likewise under the jurisdiction of that Pagan city, and a corrupt division of the Jews, that our Lord's *heel* was *bruised;* and, as if in retribution, the sword of the northern nations, and the preaching of the Gospel, subsequently brought Rome to be only a *wounded* or *bruised* head, in the year 476. But it revived in the papacy, and lives to this day. And this seems to be the earthly fulfilment; because the dragon, although a deposed power, is said in the 4th verse, still to have worship, and so has the Papacy even up to the present time.

But we must return to the more open enmity of the great beast of this chapter.

Ver. 6. "*And he opened his mouth in blasphemy against God, to blaspheme his name, and his tabernacle, and them that dwell in heaven.*"

In the preceding chapter, "the man child," who was to "rule all nations with a rod of iron," was "caught up unto God and to his throne." He therefore "*dwells in heaven.*" This then is a manifest representation of our Saviour, and we know that he is ever marked as the chief aim of Satan's enmity. But this species of enmity and blasphemy against the Saviour, the Roman power never did or could fulfil in the same degree that the Mahometan power did. The Roman empire arose before the birth of Christ, and subsequently became Christian, its heads therefore, of whatever they might have been formed, could not so *decidedly* be characterised by blasphemy, as the seven heads or divisions of the Mahometan kingdom. These last were *all founded,* and *upheld,* in *active blasphemy against God and his Christ;* whereas, notwithstanding the early Paganism of Rome, the succeeding persecution of the Christians, and the latter corruption of the Papal hierarchy, the sacerdotal department never *officially* denied Christ, or at-

tempted insidiously to degrade his holy name
beneath that of any human creature. On the contrary, the Church of Rome, as well as that of
Constantinople, however subsequently clothed in
sackcloth by human dereliction, are, and ever were,
as depositaries of the Gospel, faithful and true
descendants from the primitive Mother Church.
That of Rome was founded by the Apostles, and
that of Constantinople was a lateral delegation from
it. The primitive Mother Church was first assisted
by the emperor Antoninus Pius in 152, but may be
said to have been borne to her place of refuge on
eagle's wings, when Constantine the Great, emperor of the two wings of the Roman kingdom, in
314 put a stop to the ten persecutions, and by
edict sanctioned the Christian Church in both
departments of his empire. From this time of
legal and imperial foundation, the Eastern and
Western Churches appear to have been so predominant in Christendom, and so permanent, as to
fulfil the two symbols in the fourth of Zechariah,
where two olive trees, standing on each side of a
candlestick, (which, on the authority of our Saviour,
is the representative of a Church,) are said to be
"*the two anointed ones that stand by the Lord of the
whole earth,*" and pour "the golden oil out of
themselves." And in fact, the Churches which
have spread abroad upon the earth, and which
form the state of *Christendom,* have emanated
chiefly from those two imperially appointed churches

of the Western and Eastern departments of the Roman empire.   They are also AGAIN notified, in the eleventh of Revelations, as the *"two witnesses, the two olive trees, and the two candlesticks standing before the God of the earth."*   This information, supplied both by the Old and New Testament, makes the statement indelible.   No subsequent and fortuitous introduction of images, and other extrinsical corruptions, can at all bring those two ancient Christian trunks upon a level with the blasphemy, which was visible upon every military or sacerdotal head, that reared itself in the Moslem empire.

The eleventh chapter of Revelations appears thus to announce the two pre-eminent churches.

Ver. 3. "And I will give power unto my two witnesses, and they shall prophesy a thousand two hundred and threescore days, clothed in sackcloth.

Ver. 4. " These are the two olive trees, and the candlesticks standing before the God of the earth.

Ver. 5. "And if any *man* will hurt them, fire proceedeth out of their mouth, and devoureth their enemies : and if any *man* will hurt them, he must in this manner be killed."

The term *men*, when specifically applied, is often used in Scripture to designate the Antichristian party, and it may with the greatest degree of probability be looked upon as so meant in the above 5th verse.   Now the *men* of Mahomet's blasphemous religion conquered the chief provinces of

K

both the Eastern and Western departments of the Roman empire, and were once in Rome. Still, with all their active animosity against the Christian religion, they were never able to *hurt* either of these two *divinely* appointed Churches, which are ordained in the eleventh chapter to preach 1260 years. The Mahometan arms have for centuries surrounded the Christian Church of Constantinople, but it *continues ;* and these two pillars of Scripture truth, mentioned in both the Old Testament and the New, remain as yet standing miracles in Europe, to demonstrate to the readers of both the Old Testament and the New, that is both Jew and Christian, the truth and exactitude of prophecy, till the time "when they shall have finished their *testimony*[1]."

Bishop Newton, speaking of the Saracens, says, " They might greatly harass and *torment* both the Greek and Latin Churches, but they should not utterly extirpate the one or the other. They besieged Constantinople, and even plundered Rome, but they could not make themselves masters of either of those capital cities. The Greek empire suffered most from them. They dismembered it of Syria, and Egypt, and some other of its best and richest provinces; but they were never able to subdue and conquer the whole. As often as they besieged Constantinople they were repulsed and

---

[1] Rev. xi. 7.

defeated. They attempted in the reign of Constantine Pogonatus, A. D. 672, but their men and ships were miserably destroyed by the sea-fire invented by Calinicus; and after seven years fruitless pains, they were compelled to raise the siege, and to conclude a peace. They attempted it again in the reign of Leo Isauricus, A. D. 716; but they were forced to desist by famine and pestilence, and losses of various kinds[1]."

Thus we find that the locusts, or Saracens, issuing from the bottomless pit, were under several restrictions. "And it was commanded them that they should not hurt the grass of the earth, neither any green thing, neither any tree; but only those men which have not the seal of God in their foreheads." (Rev. ix. 4.) This limited command shows us that there were very different sorts of people dwelling upon the earth, who would be quite differently affected by the malignant efforts of the enemies of God. And it is a command which does not stand alone, for we shall find it again repeated. The prohibition not to hurt any *tree* seems also covertly to include the preservation of the two olive trees of Zechariah, and the two olive trees, and the two faithful witnesses of the eleventh chapter of Revelations. These churches are not to be hurt till the second woe, whereas the locusts rise from the bottomless pit under the first. Apparently

---

[1] Bp. Newton, vol. ii. p. 212.

K 2

the locusts are only allowed to *hurt*, that is probably proselyte, a certain party of *men*, God having
promised to keep his true servants "from the hour
of temptation which shall come upon the world."
(Rev. iii. 10.)

Ver. 5. "And there was given unto him a
mouth speaking great things and blasphemies."

Would St. John have so strongly characterised
the Roman empire as blasphemous, when there
was another empire to succeed it, which would so
much more deserve the title? This the Moslem
empire certainly did, and a perpetually blasphemous
mouth was given to it by the enforced doctrines of
the Koran. But the Romans had no direct or
specific mouth of blasphemy. Nevertheless, the
sufferings of the Christians, under the growing
usurpations of Rome, drove them to seek in the
Scriptures for some type, or symbolical account,
of the power which afflicted them. Accordingly,
having found several satanic portraits there, they,
not having a prophetic view into futurity, naturally
attributed them all to the *existing* powers, either of
Rome or the Roman Empire. And the great
beast of this chapter was adopted, among the
rest, as a portrait of the universal empire of Rome,
which it certainly not only resembled, but was
perhaps intended so to do, that the real great
antichrist might not be altogether revealed or
understood till an appointed time. According to
St. Paul, however, "When that which is perfect

is come, then that which is in part shall be done away."

When we take into our view the acknowledged consistency of prophecy, we shall see the absolute necessity that four empires of *notoriety* shall be found to have arisen in chronological order upon the site of the Metallic Image, subsequent to the time of Daniel's vision in his seventh chapter, dated as it is in the reign of Belshazzar; we ought to find that these four empires, can, by their attributes and characteristics, answer to the general description given of Daniel's four beasts, reckoning from the Lion (for reasons already given). The last empire also ought to be found capable, either of itself or by means of its horns, to reach on to the day of judgment; because the last emblem of the iron and clay kingdom, and the last (fourth) beast, are shown, by the inspired explanations concerning them, to proceed on to that time, which completes the compendiums of the Metallic Image, and of the four beasts. Moreover, the last empire educed must be found to be, in its *collective* capacity, in a *direct* state of *open rebellion against the Father and the Son of our Scriptures*, because the coetaneous explanations of the two last symbols describe them to be so; and they must be eminently Antichristian. All this, to a certain extent, the Mahometan empire fulfilled; and the remains of its antichristian profes-sors are alive to this day, and *practising* in Turkey, Persia, India, and parts of Africa, while the Roman empire has been extinct above a thousand years. It is therefore, according to Sir Isaac Newton's recommendation, to the opening views which an examination of retrospective prophecies can give, that we must resort for the unfolding of those parts, which can fill up the void space left in the compendiums, that is the void (usually left by commentators) between the extinction of the Roman empire and the day of Judgment ; and this vacuum is occasioned by not allowing the Saracenic empire to take its place in succession to the Roman, which we know it chronologically did.

CHAPTER VI.

CONTINUATION OF THE THIRTEENTH OF REVELATIONS.

THE beast, animated by the dragon's power, receives worship from all those, " whose names were not written in the book of life of the Lamb slain from the foundation of the world." (Rev. xiii. 8.)

The discrimination here made between those people whose names were written in the Lamb's book of life, and those whose names were *not* written there, discloses, incidentally indeed, but in direct, plain, and undeniable words, that there was, according to the knowledge of Heaven, a spiritual difference between the people who chose to worship the Antichristian beast, and those who declined it. This momentous information of Scripture has been authoritatively given before, and will appear again, and we dare not contradict it; but, with respect to the adoption of the Mahometan religion, (that is, the worship of the beast,) there is an admission, in the subsequent nineteenth chapter, that many were *deceived*, and our reliance upon the goodness of God teaches us to hope and believe that such will ultimately be objects of his mercy.

This beast has power "to make war with the *saints*," a term apparently adopted to distinguish the loyal adherents of the revealed God, who had received either the old or the new covenant, promulgated by him, from the worshippers of the beast, who is in open rebellion against the revealed God, from first to last. It is clear that such general rebellion as this, the people of the Roman empire never collectively fulfilled, but the people of the Mahometan empire did most *completely*. According to the mention made in the 10th verse, this was a time to exercise "the patience and the faith of the saints;" and great must have been the firmness, and the power of resistance, with which those Jews and Christians were endued, who refused and yet survived, the military and sacerdotal enforcements of the Koran, during the tyrannical and predominant course of the Saracenic empire. It had indeed been previously declared to the faithful Christian : "*Because thou hast kept the word of my patience, I also will keep thee from the hour of temptation, which shall come upon all the world, to try them that dwell upon the earth.*"

This prophetic warning and promise, delivered by the dictation of Christ himself to St. John, some hundred years before the rise of Mahometanism, must ever convince us of his superintendance over that community of people, whose " *names were written in his book of life.*" These are the people mentioned in the Ephesians, as having " *obtained an inheritance.*" (Chap. i. 11.) This information, so expressly given, is indelible; and it is openly confirmed, not by the *parable,* but by our Saviour's own *explanation* of the parable, of the wheat and the tares (Matt. xiii. 37—39); where he declares the good seed to be sown by himself, and the bad seed by Satan. Such positive passages as these, and many others of the same import, make it absolutely necessary for us to keep in mind the information, which we have clearly received, that the people, who worshipped the dragon and the beast, had no part in " the *Lamb's book of life.*" They were plainly another seed. Satan had required worship from our Saviour; he is therefore evidently ambitious of worship, and would induce or command it whenever he could; and his community of people afforded that worship, which the community of the revealed God and his Christ refused.

The enmity, foredoomed to exist between the seed of the woman and the seed of the serpent, must prevail extensively, and it forms apparently great part of the warfare and trials of this world; upon which account, it is necessary to resort to that original mandate, whenever the liquidation of this subject of prophecy is our object. Indeed,

8

without the above information, how can we account
for the great *strength* of wickedness which we see
in the world, and the extensive adherence there is
to so plain a forgery as the religion of Mahomet
exhibits ? Original sin cannot satisfactorily account
for it, because original sin was not *partial;* and
Scripture most plainly informs us that there were
a people, whose names were *not written in the
Lamb's* (that is our Saviour's) *book of life, from
the foundation of the world.* Moreover, we are
now reading a symbolical account of a direct and
palpable rebellion against him, which was visible
and well known, to all the enlightened part of the
earth, and one which must ever remain a strong
feature in the history of the world, the prophetic
types of which we are by retrospect endeavouring
to trace.

One of the earliest denunciations from the mouth
of the Deity was, that the woman, after the fall,
should be subject to a multiplied conception. This
new ordination permitted the introduction of that
seed, or of those *spirits,* whose names had never
been written in the Lamb's book of life. And the
incarnation of such is plainly exemplified in the
instances of Cain and Abel, Esau and Jacob.
Jacob was *promised seed* from heaven, while Esau
was the father of *a nation against whom the Lord
had indignation for ever;* and Scripture confirms
the fact that they were two manner of people,
born at the same time from the same womb.

Was not this a *given proof* of the multiplied conception ?

At the 10th verse of this chapter, the beast appears to decline or recede, but without undergoing death, and we know that the Saracenic empire did decline, by diminution, till it was chiefly represented by the two pre-eminent Caliphates, which were latterly regarded more as sacerdotal than temporal powers. Indeed the last descendants of the Prophet were reduced to hire foreign troops for their immediate defence, their own armies having vanished from the face of the earth.

In the preceding twelfth chapter, it was shown that a *flood* (or multitudes) was poured from the scarlet dragon's mouth after the woman (the Christian Church), but that the earth helped the woman, and the earth opened her mouth, and *swallowed up the flood that the dragon cast out of his mouth*. It is said that, " when figurative language is so plain in its designation that it cannot be mistaken, it may be received as literal." Now the earth swallowing up the flood, which the serpent cast out of his mouth, is plainly figurative of the yawning graves, which certainly did receive both the persecuting Romans and the invading Saracens. The Romans and their language disappeared first, and finally the Saracens were no more seen in any of their western conquests, where countless numbers must have fallen in war.

Knowing them, therefore, to be constituted and *persecuting* enemies of the Christian Church (the woman), we may surely apprehend the above language, which so closely describes the cause of their declining empire, to be literal.   In harmony with that supposition, we know that the Saracenic dominion vanished first from Europe, the site upon which the two anointed churches stood, which were not to be hurt by *men*, (specifically so called) till the appointed time. (Rev. xi. 4, 5.)

REVELATIONS, CHAP. XIII.

Ver. 9. "If any man hath an ear to hear, let him hear.

Ver. 10. "He that leadeth into captivity, shall go into captivity: he that killeth with the sword, must be killed with the sword. Here is the patience and the faith of the saints."

Although the above verses indicate retaliation, they do not pronounce a final doom upon the beast.   Retribution, however, being intimated, and that by the sword, may not this beast, (as the Saracenic empire certainly did) recede in a mutilated, a divided, and a wounded state ?   But power had been given to this ten horned beast to continue forty and two months.   (Rev. xiii. 5.)   It may be necessary therefore to seek for some epoch of time, from which the above beast's actual existence may in some degree be dated (always supposing him to

mean the Saracenic empire). Now, he is described
as bearing among his seven heads one that was
wounded. If this wounded head therefore represents, as according to most interpreters it does, the
head of the fallen western empire of Rome, which
recovered in the Papacy, it clearly gives to the
beast a date *subsequent* to the fall of Rome in 476.
Now history relates that the Saracenic dominion
did not begin to rise till above a century after the
fall of Rome, and we are therefore proceeding with
a strict attention to chronology.

The term of months allowed to the beast is
always understood to mean 1260 years, because
in prophetical language by days we must generally
understand years, and because no great empire
ever continued only for the space of forty and two
literal months. But the one reigning body of the
Saracenic empire did not *appear* to fulfil the term
of 1260 years; and the seeming deficiency in the
predicted space of duration may have been the
cause, which deterred some expositors from proceeding in the endeavour to find any further
correspondence between the beast of this chapter
and the empire in question. But the strict words
which describe his term, are that he shall continue
to *practise* 1260 years. At what time the Saracenic
power may be considered as deserving the name of
a *beast*, or empire, we may not be able exactly to
determine, but Mahomet himself was active as a
leader in the seventh century. In the same cen-

tury he died, leaving two branches of his race, which became the Caliphs of Persia and of Egypt. Each of these caliphs was esteemed divine by his own subjects, and each devolved his mysterious title, and whatever dignity and privilege belonged to it, formally into the hands of the Turkish power. The caliph of Persia, first, invested Togral Beg, or Tangrolipix, with the dignity of temporal vice-gerent over the Moslem world, A. D. 1057. It now remains to be shown, from the impartial statements of history, that an especially endowed commission was *also* formally transmitted into the hands of the Turks, by one of the last descendants of Mahomet in the line of the caliphs of Egypt. " One of the descendants of the caliphs of Bagdad, (Mohammed II.) on the ruin of that capital by the Moguls, had fled to Egypt; and, being the last of his sacred race, his family were treated with all the respect due to the successor of the successors of the prophet. A scion of this fallen trunk of the Abassides was found by Selim at Cairo, 1517, and conducted to Constantinople, where he maintained him at his own expense, and at his demise received from him the formal renunciation of the Caliphate. In this empty title the Turkish sovereign obtained a distinction, which secured to him and his descendants the veneration of all Mussulmans of the Sonnee sect. The posterity of this last of the Caliphs have sunk to the level of subjects ; but the spiritual influence and supremacy, derived from this

investiture, is by no means a barren privilege, even
to the present occupant of the Turkish throne[1]."

Thus it appears that there was a formal devolve-
ment of Mahometan spirit into the Turkish horn,
seated at Constantinople, once the *seat* of the
Roman emperors.   Whether then we look upon
the foregoing official renunciation, and the formal
putting into commission of the vital spirit of the
receding Saracenic empire, as a real delegation of
Antichristian power or not, we must still recognize
the two devolvements into two departments of the
Turkish government, just recited, as a licensed
measure, which can, and really does, enable them
to continue and prolong the essential *practice* of
the lately conspicuous, but now unseen, Mahometan
empire, so that it can virtually fulfil its allotted
term of 1260 years.   In fact, we know that the
authorized successors of that power, the Turks, do,
as far as they can without diminishing their taxes,
compel all people within their jurisdiction to become Mahometans, they being bound to enforce
Mahometanism by the religion itself.   Now Mahometanism is the true worship of the beast, and it
is in full *practice* in Turkey, Persia, part of the
East Indies, and part of Africa.   All this existing
and extensive rebellion against God and his Christ
being evidently within the cognizance of Scripture,
we may still look forward in St. John, and other

---

[1] Crichton's Arabia, vol. ii. p. 130.

prophetical writers, for more instructions concerning it, down to the latest times of the Christian æra.

Both the ten horns of the great beast of this chapter, and the two horns of the beast which succeeds him, appear to require a more particular investigation than they have hitherto received.

While the Saracenic empire was dominant, and reaching from Spain to Persia, including part of the late Western empire, it must have comprehended so many different states and nations, that it was as capable of affording ten horns as the previous Western empire had ever been. Is it not then more reasonable to ascribe ten horns to the living, the reigning, Saracenic empire, than to retrograde and advert to the ten horns of an extinct empire, whose wounded head, Rome, alone survived the bruising of the Northern nations. This wounded head, according to fair inference, represents the head of the Dragon, who gave his power and his strength to the beast, whereby he becomes incorporated with him, and hence may arise the great likeness between the emblems of the Roman and the Saracenic empires. 'In agreement with this, we shall find that the two-horned beast, which succeeds the combined beast and exercises his power, "causeth the earth, and them which dwell therein, to worship the *first beast, whose deadly wound was healed.*"

L

The beast with two horns.

REV. CHAP. xiii.

Ver. 11. "And I beheld another beast coming up out of the earth ; and he had two horns like a lamb, and he spake as a dragon.

Ver. 12. "And he exerciseth all the power of the first beast before him, and causeth the earth and them which dwell therein, to worship the first beast, whose deadly wound was healed.

Ver. 13. "And he doeth great wonders, so that he maketh fire come down from heaven on the earth in the sight of men.

Ver. 14. "And deceiveth them that dwell on the earth by the means of those miracles which he had power to do in the sight of the beast ; saying to them that dwell on the earth, that they should make an image to the beast, which had the wound by a sword, and did live.

Ver. 15. "And he had power to give life unto the image of the beast, that the image of the beast should both speak, and cause that as many as would not worship the image of the beast should be killed.

Ver. 16. "And he caused all, both small and great, rich and poor, free and bond, to receive a mark in their right hand, or in their foreheads."

The ten-horned beast of this thirteenth chapter

is always looked upon as the latter illustration of
Daniel's fourth beast, but this two-horned beast
has no acknowledged type in the Old Testament,
nor has it either name or date; we are therefore
without guide or sanction concerning him, further
than that he is evidently of the confederacy of the
ten-horned beast, because he exercises all his
power, and speaks like a dragon. A *beast* having
two horns must consist of three several departments, those of his two horns, and that of his own
personal state. The conjunction of the above
three is certain, yet any discrimination concerning
them is most difficult, as we do not know the
nature of the mystic connexion which subsists
between them. According to the eleventh and
seventeenth chapters, the ten-horned beast will
reascend to dominion for a short time in the latter
days; a first and second sense, therefore, may
exist in this chapter. If that is the case, the
imperfect sense being the first, we must be content with the mere shadowing out which it will
afford.

The little but important horn springing up among
the ten horns of the fourth beast, so remarkably
portrayed by Daniel, has long been a subject of
investigation, and it is interpreted as a representation of the Papacy. Apparently that little horn
exceeds the active term of the fourth beast himself, and is of so momentous a nature in his warfare
with the saints, (God's servants) that we cannot

but expect, when St. John, a Christian prophet, is here illustrating Daniel's ten-horned beast at large, that he will likewise include the little horn, which so evidently belonged to the system of the beast, and was included by Daniel in his compendious chapter. And here it is worthy of observation that Daniel, in describing his four beasts, employs only one verse each for his three first, while the fourth beast with his horns takes up twenty-one verses. After such elaboration as this, we certainly ought to prepare ourselves to meet with still greater in the elucidations of the Apocalypse, and indeed most necessarily so, because, if this beast or his horns are to reach on to the end of the world, we have reason to hope that the method by which they will thus proceed, (however little foreseen by us) will be portrayed in prophecies which are gradually to unfold as we advance in time. We look therefore earnestly here for some notice of the little horn, described by Daniel, and more especially as there has really been a little horn in the guise of Christianity, which has grievously and extensively afflicted the primitive worshippers of the true God, by enforcing idolatry upon the pure religion of Jesus Christ, and exacting odious conditions from those who professed it.

Notwithstanding all these reasons, incumbent as they manifestly appear, we now meet with the apparent cessation, or eclipse, of the great beast, without any mention of the little horn so much dwelt upon by Daniel, and which was evidently meant to proceed on to the day of Judgment. We are consequently lost in disappointment, till awakened to the consideration of a beast rising with *two* horns like those of a lamb, but speaking like a dragon, which immediately indicates his descent from, or fraternity with, the foregoing beast, which had received the dragon's *power, strength, and seal.* This renders it probable that in that part of Daniel's seventh chapter, where he gives an elaborare account of the fourth beast and his horns, there was included, in the disguise of various and unaccountable repetitions, not only a prophecy of the successive stages of the beast during his long course, (confirmed by Revelation,) but also emblems of two little horns, or one little and one peculiar horn, which would arise in different stations within the precincts of the beast. For we must remember that there were other distinguished powers in Europe besides the Papacy, and that we are now considering a *beast.* There were the Cæsars of the Eastern or Greek empire, who gave the grant of supremacy to the Pope. Among them the famous Greek fire, (which not only rose in perpendicular ascent, but likewise burnt with equal vehemence in descent,) was kept a secret above four hundred years, and was alleged to be a communication from heaven[1]. (Ver. 13.)

---

[1] There was for several hundred years a matter of notoriety and

There was the Patriarchate, and finally the Turkish horn, which became a king or sultan.   None of these are comparatively beneath the notice of

wonder attached to Constantinople, which may here be produced as deserving some observation.

It does not appear that the famous Greek fire has ever been clearly understood, but, for the purpose of annoying and intimidating their enemies, the Greeks had the ingenuity to force this wonderful fire, " through long hollow metal tubes, from the opening of which it not only rose in perpendicular ascent, but likewise burnt with equal vehemence in *descent*, or lateral progress: it was nourished and quickened by the element of water."

Mr. Gibbon thus further speaks of it. " In the two sieges, the deliverance of Constantinople may be chiefly ascribed to the novelty, the terrors, and the real efficacy, of the Greek fire. . . . The historian who presumes to analyse this extraordinary composition should suspect his own ignorance, and that of his Byzantine guides, so prone to the marvellous, so careless, and in this instance so jealous of the truth.

" This important art was preserved at Constantinople, as the palladium of the state.   The composition of the Greek fire was concealed with the most jealous scruple, and the terror of the enemies was increased and prolonged by their ignorance and surprise. . . . *The secret was confined above four hundred years to the Romans of the East.*"

" In the treatise of the administration of the Empire, the royal author suggests the answers and excuses that might best elude the indiscreet curiosity and importunate demands of the barbarians.   They should be told that the mystery of the Greek fire *had been revealed* by *an Angel*, to the first and greatest of the Constantines, with a sacred injunction that this gift of heaven, this peculiar blessing of the Romans, should never be communicated to any foreign nation."   Gibbon, vol. x. chap. 52.

Was not this assuming that the fire came down from heaven ?

prophecy: they have had much to do in the Christian warfare, and are not likely to be left unnoted by the last Christian prophet, St. John. More encouraged then by the hope of gaining even a glimpse of an object worthy of deep attention, than deterred by the fear of failure, we must again turn to the paths of the Old Testament, where the obscured prototypes dwell. The Old Testament is in general remarkable for comprehensive yet concise emblems, and pithy narratives. We are compelled therefore to acknowledge surprise, when it so far departs from that usual method, as to give in one chapter, (the seventh of Daniel,) such apparently unnecessary repetitions as must awaken expectation of something more than is apparent.

In the first account given by Daniel of *his* vision of the fourth beast, in the 20th verse of his seventh chapter, the beast's horns are said to be in his *head*; and Daniel *considered* them, so that there is no mis-statement to be apprehended. The ten horns were apparently in his first estate; and there can be scarcely a doubt that the little horn, which begins to be described at the 8th verse, and is continued to the 21st, means the Papacy, because the papal influence and power really did root up three horns or states of Italy, and, under the sanction of Pepin and Charles the Great, annexed them to Peter's patrimony. This seems a decisive fulfilment on the part of the Pope. And here we must call the attention of the reader to the fact that the same little horn, which we think portrays him, is distinguished by *having eyes like a man,* whatever that expression may mean; while that distinguishing feature of him is omitted after the 20th verse. At the 21st and 22nd verses the subject, or at least that part of it, seems finished. Nevertheless, at the 23rd verse, the angel *unasked* again begins an apparent repetition of that, which had unnecessarily been related two or three times before. Upon a closer inspection, however, it will be found that the description is *not* exactly the same. At the 20th verse the ten horns are said to be in the beast's *head,* but, in this *last* relation by the angel, the ten horns are particularized as ten *kings* that SHALL arise out of the beast's *body* or empire. It is added, moreover, in the same 24th verse, that "*another,* (which, consistently with the context, must be another king,) shall rise after them, *and he shall be diverse from the first and he shall subdue three kings.*" Now the Pope is not a king, nor did he ever subdue three kings properly so called. The Lombards were conquered by the arms of France, which the Pope had called into Italy to protect and assist him; and, after the conquest of Lombardy and other states, the kings of France formally made them over to the Pope, and thus did the uprooted horns fall before him. The Pope, moreover, never "*spake great words against the most High;*" he cannot therefore be the ori-

ginal of the eleventh horn of the 24th and
25th verses, though he may be the original of
the 8th and 20th verses, as a *little* horn, before
which, it is to be observed, three of the FIRST
horns were plucked up by the roots. There never
has been any settled opinion about the ten horns of
the Roman empire, and, even if there had, the
event of the ten-horned dragon, (after his fall in
476,) giving his power and strength to the newly
risen blasphemous beast of this chapter, must un-
settle them, as we know not to what extent the
dragon's gift reached.

According to Bishop Newton, the power of the
Pope as a horn, or temporal prince, was not established till the eighth century. (Newton on the
Prophecies, vol. i. p. 282.) If that calculation of the
Bishop is correct, the power of the Papacy did not
fulfil the character of Daniel's *little horn*, till above
three hundred years after the fall of the Western
empire of Rome. Leo the Ninth, who lived in the
eleventh century, is mentioned as the first Pope
who maintained an army. Mr. Gibbon says that,
" Rome acquiesced under the absolute dominion of
the Popes about the same time that Constantinople
was enslaved by the Turkish arms." (Decline and
Fall, vol. xii. p. 257.) This shows how *late* there
was a confraternal movement in the two seven-
hilled cities of Rome and Constantinople, the two
lamb-like horns of which have formed the empire
of Christendom. Yet the Pope of the first, and

the Patriarch of the latter, do not of themselves
seem equal to fulfil the character of the beast with
two horns like a lamb but speaking like a dragon ;
for, although the Papacy has been more *stout*, and
spoken greater *words*, and massacred millions of
Protestants, the Patriarchate has merely rivalled it
by preaching the same lamb-like religion, and yet
practising idolatry.   A much stronger exemplification of personal Antichristianity may therefore be
looked for; and leaving the Pope to the ample
description which Bishop Newton has given of the
image which he (the Pope) presents of the tyranny
and vices of the Western Roman emperors, we
must turn to the Eastern division, where there is
another prophetic land-mark of seven hills.   And
here it is proper to observe, that, until we hear of
the cessation of the two-horned beast, we must
consider the first ten-horned beast as still practising by his means, because he raises " an image" to
him, which can "both speak, and cause that as
many as will not worship *the beast* shall be killed."
The worship of the beast with the wounded head
is equally required with authority.   The three
subjects upon earth which we may imagine to be
foreshown by the two-horned beast, do not appear
to us to be connected.   What indeed can be more
apparently distinct than the Papacy, the Patriarchate, and the Turkish sultan?   Still we are
informed that there are three living powers, called
in the Apocalypse the dragon, the beast, and the

false prophet; and although we may not be able to assign them appropriately to their earthly states, the complex subject naturally leads us to recollect the description, given by the Apocryphal Esdras, of an Antichristian eagle with three heads, that for a season ruled in the earth with much oppression, when after a time he saw that the three heads were joined together.   (4 Esdras, ch. xi.)

In Daniel's last empire a division is foretold, but we know not whether the division is a local or a spiritual division, and therefore it is with much apprehension of erring conclusions that we venture on to the Eastern department of the late Roman empire, where the people of the Patriarchate had so far departed from the purity of the primitive Christians as to become great *transgressors*.   And this brings us to the consideration of an Antichristian power, which appears to approach as an appointed scourge, and is, in the repetitions of the eighth chapter, called first at the 9th verse, " a little horn which waxed exceeding great," and subsequently at the 23rd verse " a king," which is a natural consequence after waxing great. This will occasion the examination of one of the four divisions of Alexander's broken kingdom, that in which Constantinople stands, because in that division a part of the Turkish power first arose a little horn, but afterwards became a king or sultan.

DANIEL, CHAP. viii.

Ver. 8. " Therefore the he goat waxed very great : and when he was strong, the great horn was broken; and for it came up four notable ones towards the four winds of heaven.

Ver. 9. " And out of one of them came forth a little horn, which waxed exceeding great, toward the east and toward the pleasant land.

Ver. 10. " And it waxed great, even to the host of heaven; and it cast down some of the host and of the stars to the ground, and stamped upon them.

Ver. 11. " Yea, he magnified himself even to the prince of the host, and by him the daily sacrifice was taken away, and the place of his sanctuary was cast down.

Ver. 12. " And an host was given him against the daily sacrifice by reason of transgression, and it cast down the truth to the ground; and it practised and prospered."

Ver. 21. " And the rough goat is the king of Grecia : and the great horn that is between his eyes is the first king.

Ver. 22. " Now that being broken, whereas four stood up for it, four kingdoms shall stand up out of the nation, but not in his power.

Ver. 23. " And in the latter time of their kingdom, when the transgressors are come to the full,

a king of fierce countenance, and understanding
dark sentences, shall stand up.

Ver. 24. And his power shall be mighty, but
not by his own power : and he shall destroy won-
derfully, and shall prosper, and practise, and shall
destroy the mighty and the holy people.

Ver. 25. " And through his policy also he shall
cause craft to prosper in his hand ; and he shall mag-
nify himself in his heart, and by peace shall destroy
many : he shall also stand up against the prince
of princes : but he shall be broken without hands."

The Turkish horn, which at first arose small in
Grecia, appears by " waxing great" to have attained
from thence all the points of situation marked out
in the above eighth chapter.   It "waxed great towards the South," where it subdued Egypt; and
spread " towards the East," till it reached the
Tigris, and included the foundations of ancient
Babylon, the once golden head.   The next country hinted at in the prophecy is " the pleasant
land."   This apparently was an intermediate country, and notable in its state; and we therefore
readily acknowledge in it the Holy Land, where
the Turks have long been proud masters.   Among
these various conquests, the Turks must inevitably
have " subdued three kings," according to the
24th verse of Daniel's seventh chapter, wherein
I have presumed that there was a covert prophecy
of the Turkish king, rather than an useless, and
apparently inapplicable, repetition concerning the

Papal little horn that "had eyes like the eyes of a man."

This apparent fulfilment on the part of the Turkish king, who exists at this day, (if it be considered well founded), will perhaps incline the reader to recognize the before mentioned three several powers in the two-horned beast; but in no part of the eighth chapter of Daniel does the Turkish power seem more accurately described than in the 24th and 25th verses.

Ver. 24. "And his power shall be mighty, but not by his own power."

In the first place, the Turks are foreigners in Greece, where the natives still form the basis of the kingdom.

Ver. 25. "And through his policy also he shall cause craft to prosper in his hand."

By policy and craft the Sultan has waxed exceeding great, yet great only as an extrinsical image, the essence of whose sacerdotal power was, as before related, devolved upon him by the formal renunciation of the two last of the Caliphs; and this transfer of religious power must be esteemed as a delegated power, rather than the Sultan's "*own power*." The Turks also are chiefly protected and defended by auxiliary troops and Janizaries, who are paid by exactions levied upon the natives of the soil, as is thus expressed by Guthrie. "The riches drawn from the various provinces of this empire must be immense. The revenues arise from the customs, and a variety of taxes, which *fall chiefly on the Christians.*"

In further confirmation that this horn does not act by his " *own power,*" it is said that the Turkish Sultan himself trembles before the Ulemah. By the late accounts of Sir James Porter, who resided at the Porte in quality of Ambassador from his Britannic Majesty, it appears that "the rigours of that despotic government are considerably moderated by the power of religion. For, though in this empire there is no hereditary succession to property, the rights of individuals may be rendered fixed and secure by being annexed to the Church. Even Jews and Christians may in this manner secure the enjoyment of their lands to the latest posterity; and so sacred and inviolable has this law been held, that there is no instance of an attempt on the side of the prince to trespass on, or reverse it. Neither does the observance of this institution altogether depend on the superstition of the Sultan. He knows that any attempt to violate it would shake the foundation of his throne, which is solely supported by the laws of religion. Were he to transgress these laws, he would become an infidel, and cease to be the lawful sovereign."

But, "*through his policy, he doth cause craft to prosper in his hand.*" By craft, and by enforcing their religion, the Mahometan power is still in full practice.

We return to the chapter of Revelations which we are now considering.

Ver. 15. " And he had power to give life unto the *image* of the beast."

The image of an empire must be extensive, and so is the prevalence of the Mahometan religion. If, therefore, the delegation from the successors of Mahomet, is looked upon as having given vitality to the sacerdotal power of the Turks, the Mahometan beast may still be looked upon as in practice, although unrecognized as an empire. If these things are so, the remains of the beast are now practising, according to the gift of the dragon, in the Roman seat at Constantinople. In this unnoted manner, although narrated and symbolized in the Apocalypse, and described and accounted for by our own historians, was brought about, at different periods, that transfer of *power*, seat, and authority, which was mentioned at the 2nd verse, of this chapter, and which is the *Image* of Mahometanism, that we now see *practising* in the old Roman seat of the Cæsars at Constantinople.

It has already been stated, that all the greater prophets show that Esau, Edom, or Seir, will be in action in the last days. Esau is recorded to have had three wives; therefore, whether obvious or obscured, some of his Canaanitish and pagan descendants by them must reach on to that time. His grandson by his eldest son is, in the thirty-sixth

of Genesis, 15th verse, styled Duke Omar. Now
Omar, one of the earliest Caliphs, is stated to have
been one of the most rapid conquerors by the sword,
that ever spread desolation upon the face of the
earth. In a few years he subdued Egypt, Persia,
Arabia, Mesopotamia, Syria, and Jerusalem, in
which city he built a mosque. Was this like a
son of Ishmael, the wild man of the desert; or was
it like a son of Esau, who was to "*live by his
sword*," and at some period to have dominion?
The name of Omar is also perpetuated in one of
the Mahometan sects. The information that Esau,
or Edom, will be active as an adversary in the last
days, gives us fair warrant to seek after some visible
proofs of the existence of that party in the present
period of the world. But where shall the search
begin? Idumea has lost even its Grecian name;
Petra and its dependant cities are depopulated;
and although the prophecy of Zechariah allows the
red horses and their rider to walk to and fro in the
earth, and the learned Jews trace *Edom* to Rome,
still, according to the expression of Mr. Gibbon,
"there is not a Roman left visible to the legisla-
tive eye." The dominion of the Saracens has also
vanished from the sight, but the Antichristian
engine of its spiritual power, we have seen, was
most formally transmitted by two documents,
(like an inheritance to an heir), into the hands of
the Turks. They are, we repeat, a mysterious
people of doubtful origin, unlike in their persons to

M

the Tartar race from which they were supposed to
have sprung.   When they first emerged from the
North, they bore the title of Turcomans, or wan-
dering and banished men; but whether they had
previously borne that appellation to the North, and
afterwards returned with it, cannot now be ascer-
tained.   Philip of Mornay is said to have given
good reasons for the belief that they originated in
Arabia.   The immense tracts of Arabia Petræa and
Syria can allow of this; and their bearing more
resemblance to the Southern than to the Northern
inhabitants of Asia also favours the supposition.
But, wherever acquired, as soon as they became
conquerors, they discarded the name they brought
with them, and assumed that of Othmans, which
they still bear with the greatest degree of haughti-
ness.   They not only oppress the Jews and Christians, from whom they draw their sustenance, with
great cruelty, but evince constant hostility and
enmity towards them.   It was foretold that Esau
should live by the *sword.*   This the Turks have
always done.   Esau was at some period to have
a dominion, and this they have acquired by the
sword.   They are interpreted by our best commentators to be the four angels, or Sultans, which
are said, in the ninth of the Apocalypse, to have
been " bound in," that is, within, " the great river
Euphrates," which were " prepared to *slay* the
third part of men;" and we know that the Sultan
characteristically bears the title of the *man-slayer.*

Can all this be accidental? The self-appropriated
title proves the natural taste of this people for war
and carnage. Certain it is that the Othmans have
ever been looked upon as instruments in the hands
of Providence, and it is a striking coincidence that
their own conceptions concur with those of the
Christians in the apprehension that they are come
into Europe only for a limited time. In the fine
country, to which they have attained, they proceed
like tenants at will, who have no interest in its
ultimate prosperity. Depopulation, cruelty, and
rapine, have marked their steps ever since they
came. Mr. Dallaway, in his account of Constantinople, mentions that " a prophecy obtains among
the Turks that the imperial city will one day be
required by the Christians, and that, from this
motive, a fashion is prevalent among their men of
rank of choosing their graves at Scutari, that they
may not become subject to their enemies even in
death, for Asia is looked upon as the patrimony of
the Mahometans[1]."

As we are now in the nineteenth century, it is
necessary we should be aware, that the chronological chapters of the Apocalypse, as they draw
towards the conclusion, will give only such emblems
and narratives, as can exhibit the changes which
the long course of so many hundred years have
made. Yet, in these subsequent emblems and

.

---

[1] Dallaway's Constantinople, p. 155.

narratives, however necessarily altered, we must still expect to find such an obvious resemblance and connexion with the foregoing portraits and narratives, as will afford a perceptible chain of descent from one to the other, though it will certainly require constant attention fully to understand and appreciate them.

One of these *latter* portraits next comes under our consideration, and it seems to represent some of the existing circumstances of the world, which appear to be leading to the last scenes of the Apocalypse. The mechanism, or fabric of that Revelation, however, appears to be in some of its parts as yet inscrutable to us; besides which, the first and second sense may prevail where we are insensible of it. We, cannot, therefore be certain of more than a shadowing out of things, and a resemblance of that which is more perfectly to appear. *" We know in part, and we prophesy in part, but when that which is perfect is come, then that which is in part shall be done away."*

The vision and narrative given in the following chapter, being delivered by one of the angels which pour out the *last plagues,* marks the lateness of the period to which it belongs, and the situation of its symbols.

REVELATIONS, CHAP. Xvii.

Ver. 3. " So he carried me away in the spirit into

the wilderness : and I saw a woman sit upon a scarlet-coloured beast, full of names of blasphemy, having seven heads and two horns."

This being "*full of the names of blasphemy*," points more *certainly* at the professors of the Mahometan religion than at any other. And, as every mosque utters blasphemy on the seven hills of Constantinople, to what station can we so justly attribute the scarlet coloured beast as to the image empire of the Mahometan Turks, who received a formal delegation of that RED spiritual power ?

Genesis, chap. xxxvi. "Esau is Edom," that is, according to the context of Scripture, *red*. Adverting then to the several intimations of Genesis, Zechariah, and the Revelations, concerning the relation which subsists between the scarlet colour, and the Satanic confederacy, we cannot doubt that the scarlet beast of this *latter* chapter relates to Edom. And this, in accordance with the context of the Old and New Testament, shows that Esau, Seir, or *Edom*, will be in action in the last days. Even in the present day, the Mahometan Turk, like the Phantom or Image of the Saracenic beast, is seated upon the seven heads or hills of Constantinople ; where the woman, being apparently the aggregate of the three Antichristian powers, is, according to the symbolic method of Scripture, called a city, that is, the city of congregated wickedness ; while the term *mother*, added to her name

of *Babylon,* carries us back to the prototype fifth
chapter of Zechariah, in which it is shown that
wickedness was first settled in the land of *Shinar.*
Here Babylon was built soon after the flood, and
from hence, Isaiah foretold (chap. xiv. ver. 29, 31.)
that a power, originally springing from the *serpent's
root at Babylon,* would afterwards come from the
north, and dissolve the state of Palestine, which
the Romans did in the year 70.

It also appears, in this seventeenth chapter of
Revelations, that the aggregate beast, (the dragon,
the beast, and the false prophet,) will again rise
into power for a short time. This is the second
direct mention of that revival. The first mention
is in the eleventh chapter, in which it is said, that,
after the faithful witnesses have finished their testimony, " *The beast that ascendeth out of the bottomless pit, shall make war against them, and shall overcome them, and kill them.*" A dissolution of the
hierarchy of the two imperially founded churches
of Rome and Constantinople, may be necessary in
order to separate their faithful spirits from their
corrupt bodies. This is a disjunction we know that
our own souls and bodies are to undergo, when the
spirit which God gave is to be freed by death from
our corrupt flesh, and rise fruit of the resurrection,
as it appears that the spirits of these two faithful
witnesses will do. Neither the Western nor the
Eastern Church has yet been disfranchised, so that
the period here meant must be a late one ; and the

8

14th verse of the eleventh chapter confirms this statement by adding "that the second woe is past; and, behold, the third woe cometh quickly." The third woe begins the consummation of the prophetic scheme, and thus again, in part, dates the lateness of the time in which the risen beast will re-appear.

But the most certain intelligence which we derive concerning the future, from this seventeenth chapter, is that, during the last great conflicts, the three Antichristian spirits appear, under the Divine influence, to act against each other, fulfilling thus our Saviour's prophetic declaration that " *every house or city divided against itself, shall not stand* [1]."

In the sixteenth chapter of Revelations also, at the 19th verse, it is stated that, previous to the fall of Babylon, " the great city was divided into three parts."

The " *mark of the beast*" is no slight matter, that may be passed over as figurative. It is again brought forward in the fourteenth chapter, and the *reception* of the " *mark*," which we must interpret as the religion of the beast, is there stated to be the greatest crime before God. Nor can we imagine a greater than that a Christian should become a Mahometan. Such a gulf of destruction, however, is plausibly laid open by every preacher of universal toleration, or rather of universal indif-

---

[1] Matt. xii. 25.

ference.   And this shows how necessary it may
soon be to warn the young and the unwary against
the adoption of such a vain, unauthorised, and
sometimes ill-intentioned opinion.

It would no doubt be more agreeable to modern
indifference, to modern benevolence, and also to a
really kind and friendly feeling towards the worthy
individuals who may be found among our Roman
Catholic brethren, to pass over every further mention that can reflect upon papistical practices.   But
prophecy must be viewed with reference to that
which has actually passed, and is still passing, in
the world.   When therefore we see the most enlightened individuals of the Romish persuasion
still persisting in the retention of images, in
defiance of an *explicit and strict command,* can we
do otherwise than perceive, that such disobedience,
(which appears to equal that of Adam,) must proceed from delusion [1] ?   Let us however remember
that it is such a delusion, as may easily be incul-
cated and enforced upon an unsuspecting people,
born and brought up in a situation, where the
dragon's voice speaks with parental authority in
the lamb's horn.   Such subjects of the dragon's
powerful deceptions, while they remain innocent of

---

[1] " He feedeth on ashes : a deceived heart hath turned him
aside, that he cannot deliver his soul, nor say, Is there not a lie
in my right hand ?" This describes the Roman Catholic, who
denies that he worships Images, although he will rather die than
give them up.

our blood, we must ever hope are objects of God's mercy and care.

But the millions of martyrs sacrificed at the shrine of an intolerant superstition, their sufferings in the cause of pure and undefiled religion, their widows and their orphans given up as a prey to the demon of fanaticism, must never be forgotten, lest we should blindly, and unwittingly, consent to see the same undying power raised up again. Even a child of ten years of age, if educated with ordinary care, is indued with sufficient judgment to see and comprehend the offence there must be in breaking an express *commandment* of God.   And if, in defence of the papal usurpations, any stress is laid upon our Saviour's casual mention of a *rock* in his address to St. Peter, in the sixteenth chapter of St. Matthew, let it be remembered, that, in the 23rd verse of the *same* chapter, *" he turned and said unto Peter, Get thee behind me, Satan: thou art an offence unto me: for thou savourest not the things that be of God, but those that be of men."* These words are not equivocal, but more express than those upon which the Roman Catholics dwell so much.

To the above may be added our certain knowledge that the principles of the Papacy do nothing towards cleansing the peculiar corruption of morals in Italy.   This alone may convince us that it is not *holy*.   It is the part of Protestants, therefore, to read the Scriptures carefully for themselves, and silently but firmly to determine upon a strict obedience to their discriminating declarations, as they become gradually visible. At the same time, they should never either hurt, or bear ill will to, the adverse party, because they cannot know the deluded spirit from the active agent. Nevertheless the iron and the clay are not to mix although they are mingled.

REVELATIONS, CHAP. xiii.

Ver. 17. "And that no man might buy or sell, save he that had the mark, or the name of the beast, or the number of his name.

Ver. 18. " Here is wisdom. Let him that hath understanding count the number of the beast : for it is the number of a man ; and his number is six hundred, threescore and six."

We are told in Scripture that no prophecy is of private interpretation. The man here indicated, therefore, cannot be a private man, but one of notoriety both before Heaven and earth. The man, who raised up the Mahometan empire in rebellion against God and his Christ, is certainly the most remarkable man that we know of; and he answers to the description in the text. The name Mahomet, when written in Greek, as the Apocalypse was, contains the number 666. Moametic [1].

[1] The Romanists, in explaining the Book of Revelations, insist that the religion of Mahomet is pointed out by the predicted

With respect to the congeniality of the dragon, the beast, and the false prophet, they are not only classed together in the 13th verse of the sixteenth chapter of Revelations, but the last verse of this chapter may be found to apply to all three. The number **666** has long been adjudged to the Roman horn, but (as has been just shown) appears also clearly to belong to the individual *man* Mahomet, and may be appropriated to his *image* in the eastern power at Constantinople, as an image includes the attributes of its prototype.

Finally, the image of a great empire must like its original be extensive, and so is the prevalence of the Moslem religion. The question therefore, may reasonably be asked, " What other fulfilment is there of the *image* of *an empire,* if the widely extended remains of the worship of Mahomet do not exhibit it ?"   And when we reflect upon those

---

Antichrist; and they have explained that mystical number 666, which has been so variously unravelled, and is expressly said to be the number of a man, or the number of the name of a man, to apply to the name of Mahomet, which, when expressed in the Greek, in which language the Apocalypse was written, is Mahometic, or Moametic, as Euthymius, and the Greek historian, Zonares, and Cedrenus write it. The letters which compose this word, according to the Greek numeration, are thus—

M	O	A	M	E	T	I	Σ
40	70	1	40	5	300	10	200

666

Bellarmine Pastorini's (Bishop Walmesly's) History of the Church, p. 366.

remains, are we not irresistibly led to say, " It is the image, it is the *beast, which was, and is not, and yet is ?*"

It may be proper to mention that several sentiments of this book, though not acknowledged at the time, have been taken from a late publication, little known, entitled, " A New Interpretation of a part of the third chapter of Genesis."

THE END.

GILBERT & RIVINGTON, Printers, St. John's Square, London.